PUTTING PUNCH

IN THE

PARABLES

Ten Stories That Bring the Words OF JESUS to Life Today

LIZ KIMMEL

ISBN 979-8-9911769-0-3

Scriptures taken from the HOLY BIBLE, NEW LIVING TRANSLATION, Copyright © 1996, 2004, 2007 by Tyndale House Foundation,. Used by permission of Tyndale House Publishers, Inc., Carol Stream, Illinois 60188. All rights reserved. Used with permission.

Photo credits are listed at the back of the book.

Printed in the United States of America.

Published by Liz Kimmel: WordWright
St. Paul, Minnesota

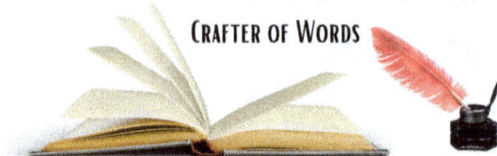

LIZ KIMMEL: WORDWRIGHT
CRAFTER OF WORDS

CONTENTS

A PARABLE
OF THE PLANTS

A planter plowed his field in preparation for the crop he planned to produce.

With his property primed, he proceeded to pace each row in the patterned patch.

Dipping his palm into a pouch, he grasped a portion of the petite and precious particles and propelled them toward a particular spot. The planter failed to perceive that his aim was not always precise.

Some of his product peppered the path that ran parallel to the plot. The sparrows, woodpeckers, and plovers pinched and plundered the misplaced seeds with pleasure.

A portion plopped onto paltry pieces of superficial dirt interspersed with pebbles. The sprouts appeared to perform well primarily. They sprung up promptly but then drooped and perished just as speedily in the parching sun.

Others fell into a precarious position among prickly spikes, whose spines and points suppressed any possibility of proliferation. They, too, expired.

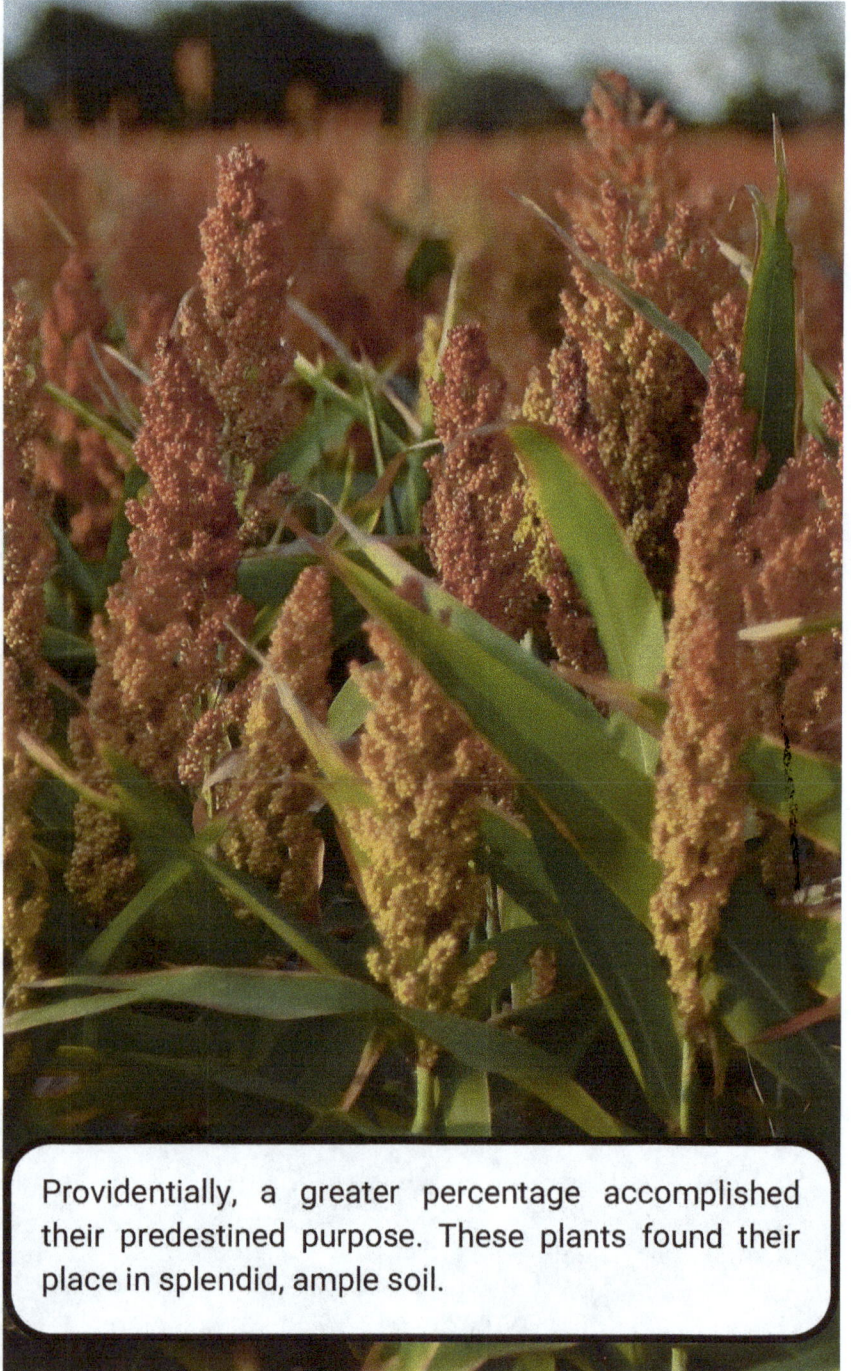

Providentially, a greater percentage accomplished their predestined purpose. These plants found their place in splendid, ample soil.

The payoff for the planter was plenteous. The perks for his persistence in this process included a plethora of produce that propagated far past his previous expectations.

These express points explain this parable.
Pay attention.

- Keep your eyes peeled so your prize is not appropriated by pilferers.

- Plunge your roots deep so you don't capitulate to persecution's power.

- Depend on your Papa when in predicaments that want to plague and overpower you.

- Persevere and perceive the penetrating truths of the Gospel.

Expect your fruit to multiply exponentially. The profusion in your pantry can be passed on and poured out to people you meet. And the promises of our Papa and his passion for all people will prevail.

THE SON
WHO STRAYED

A self-centered son spoke selfishly to his sire. "My sibling is too scared to say something, but I aspire to see the world. Settle your estate now, and split your savings between your sons. I refuse to sit still until you succumb to your final sleep.

The father stated his assent, doing as his youngest son requested. The son swiftly stuffed his suitcase until it almost burst and set off for distant places.

At first it was amusing and pleasant. But he squandered his vast sum in loose living with sly and sneaky friends. Soon, all the silver was spent. His purse was used up and his stomach was starving.

He secured a position with a local citizen and spent his days feeding slop to the man's swine. Even this disgusting mess seemed savory to the son.

Upon coming to his senses, he perceived the stupidity of his stratagem. "Even my father's servants have snacks to spare, and I am suffering starvation. If I hustle back to his place, it's feasible that he might have a spot where I can serve."

During the boy's absence, the sire was sad. But his spirit skipped for joy as he saw his son advancing from a great distance. He started toward him, swiftly closing the gap and scurrying to meet the son for whom his love had never lessened.

"I'm so sorry," the son sobbed. "I've sinned against you and against heaven. I don't deserve to be your son."

But the sire summoned the servants. "Snap to it! Bring the best suit in the house and sandals for his sore tootsies. Get a signet ring to place on his hand. And start the steaks sizzling on the stove. We're going to celebrate. My son was lost, but now he is rescued!"

The senior son was spitting mad about all the fuss and ruckus in the house. "I've slaved for you all these years and never once refused to do a single thing you asked! Where was my special feast? This stupid second son of yours comes back after sinful splurging on drunkenness and excess. And you swing for the social soiree of the season. I'm so confused!"

The wise father said softly, "You stayed. You were steadfast in your trust, and we had sweet times side by side. Celebrate with me the restoration of this one who has been so lost."

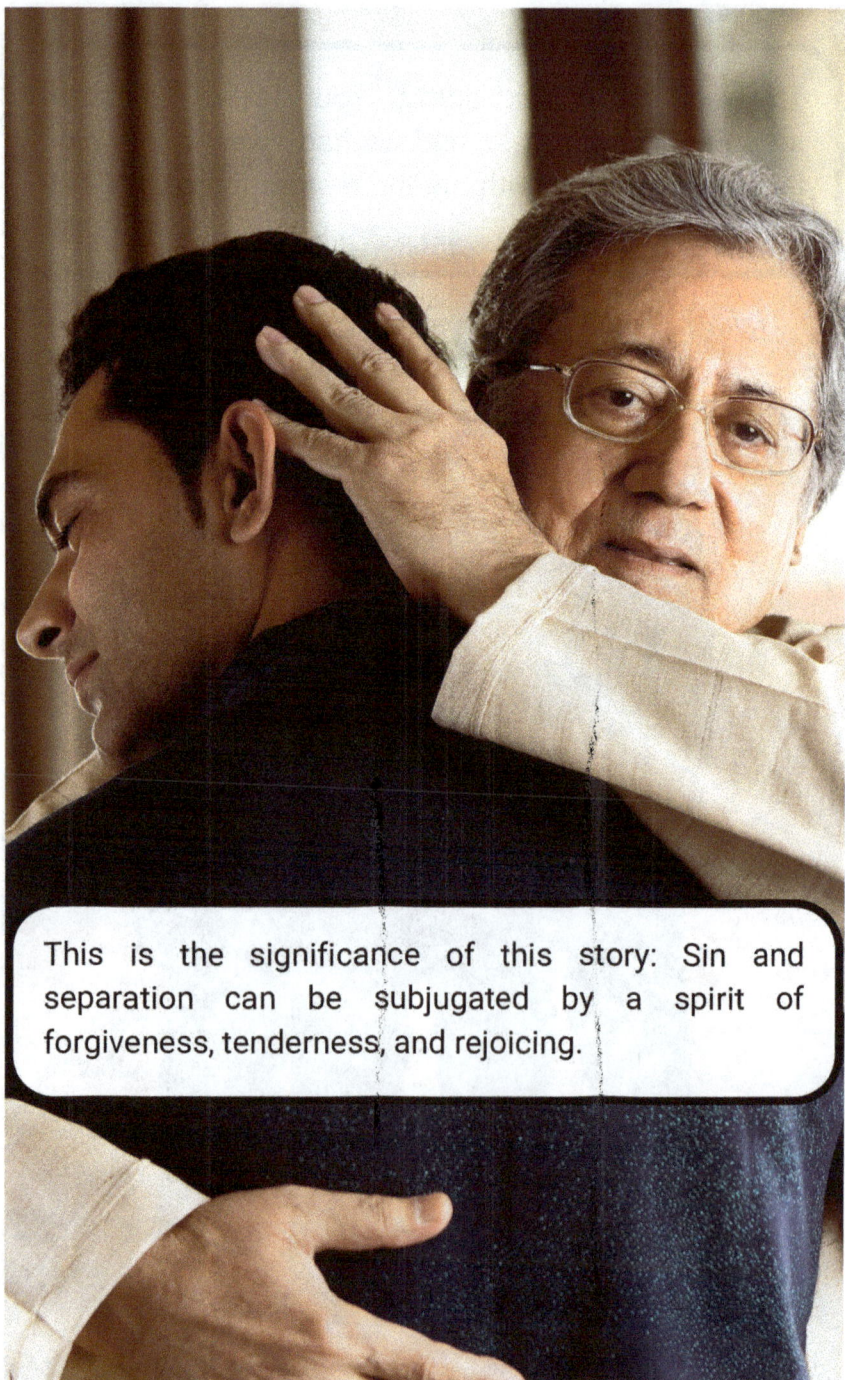

This is the significance of this story: Sin and separation can be subjugated by a spirit of forgiveness, tenderness, and rejoicing.

THE LAW LOOKS AT LOVE AND LIFE

As a learner of religious law listened to the Lord one day, he grilled Him about eternal life. "In plain language, how do I conclusively latch onto it?"

MIND

HEART

STRENGTH STRENGTH

SOUL SOUL

[Lord:] "Tell me how the law explains it."

[Learner:] "Bottom line is, love the Lord with all of yourself intellectually, physically, spiritually. And also, love other fellows just like you love yourself."

[Lord:] "Flawless! Do this, and live."

But the pupil wanted to validate his way of life and appealed for supplementary details. "Tell me exactly which lads and ladies I must love - those who live across the lane, down the line, or far afield? Those who look like me, reflect like me, believe like me? Reveal the level of love that the law applauds."

This was an excellent place to tell a parable.

A local bloke was on a long stroll, not having wheels or a mule to lessen the length of his travel time. He allotted several hours to get to his planned location.

Sadly, he was assaulted by outlaws. They stole all his clothing and pelted and pummeled him until his life was nearly lost. They were untroubled by their cruel violence and left him alone in the elements.

A religious leader whose plans for the day led him along the same lane only gave a fleeting glance at the lump of flesh lying in this vulnerable place. He looked away and quickly shuffled to the lee side of the hill.

A temple laborer also traveled past. He leaned in to look more closely at the unlucky lad. But his obligations and schedule were more vital to him than helping the helpless. He left without looking back.

A little while later a lone mule came close, led by someone that lots of locals looked upon as a loafer, a louse, even a low-life loser.

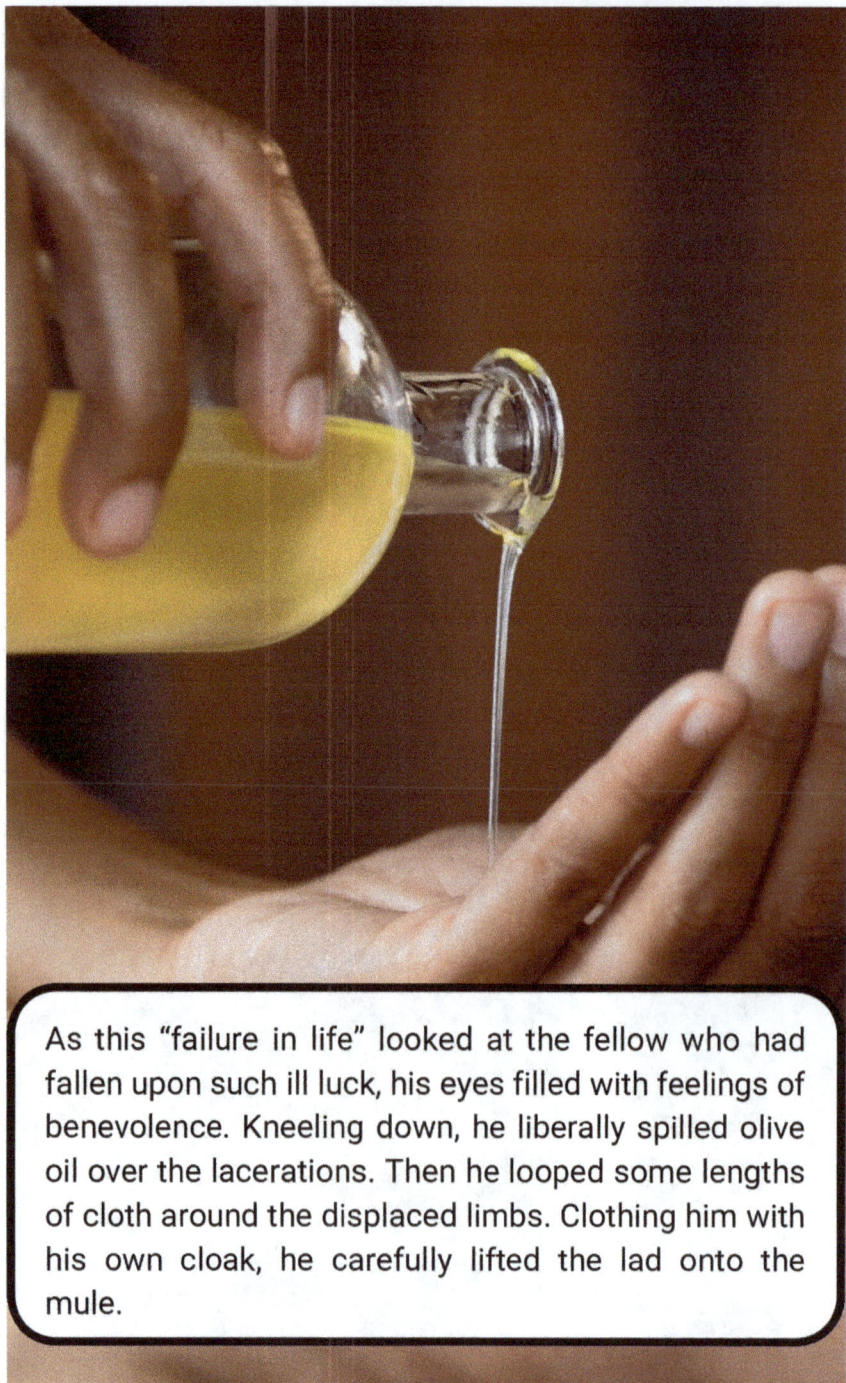

As this "failure in life" looked at the fellow who had fallen upon such ill luck, his eyes filled with feelings of benevolence. Kneeling down, he liberally spilled olive oil over the lacerations. Then he looped some lengths of cloth around the displaced limbs. Clothing him with his own cloak, he carefully lifted the lad onto the mule.

When they pulled up to the hotel, the loving helper settled his new pal into a flat and paid for his lodging.

He shelled out the silver needed for shelter and told the hotel clerk, "Look out for him. Let me know if the bill swells. I'll settle up when I circle back."

[Lord:] Who illustrated love to the fallen man?"

[Learner:] "The one who displayed goodwill."

[Lord:] "Absolutely! Now go, and live likewise."

THE SHEPHERD AND THE SHEEP

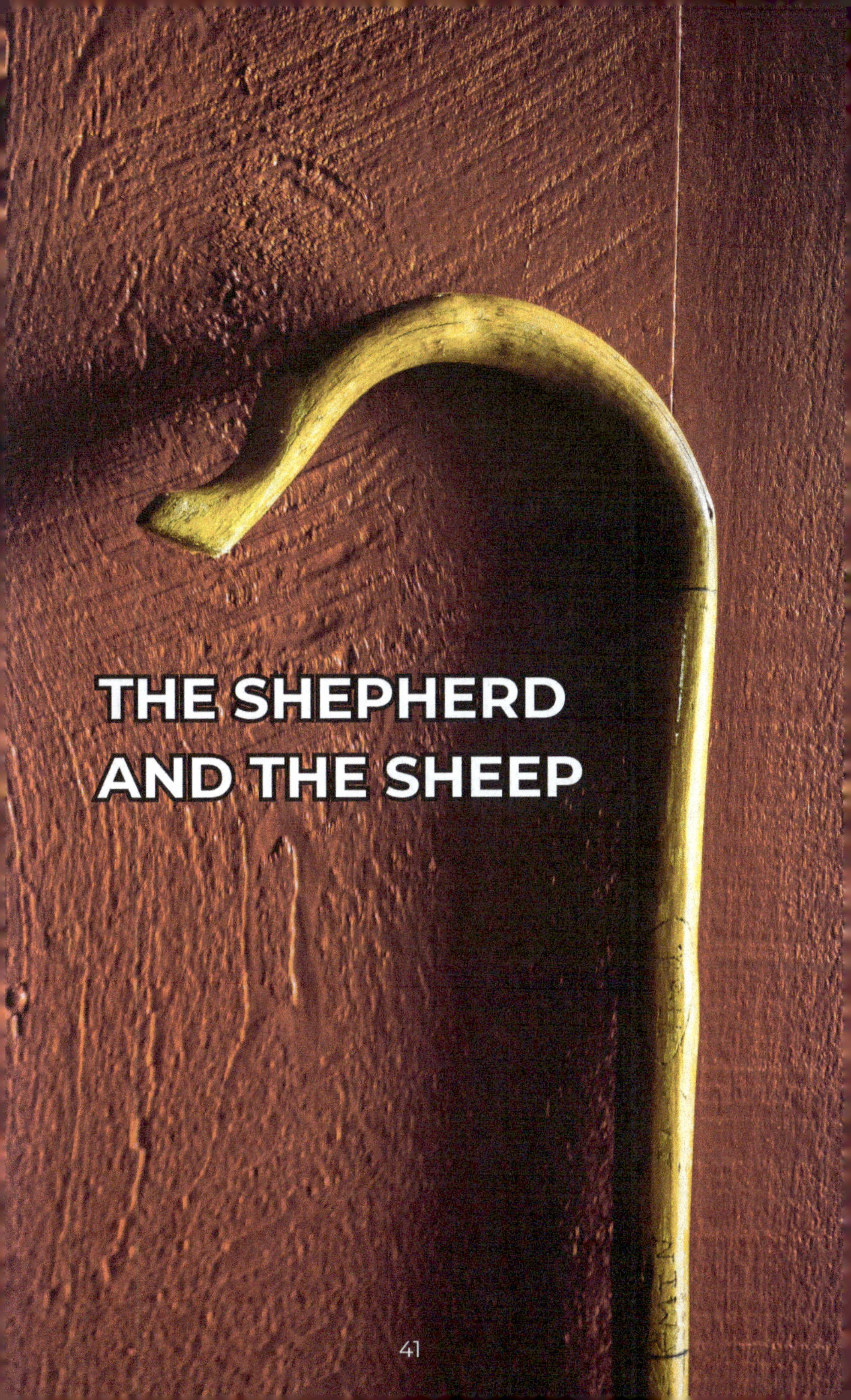

Tax-collection officials and other shameful sinners were often seen in association with Jesus. They appreciated the discussions he led. They sometimes even shared nourishment together.

This action caused the "sheriffs" of the worship faction to caution him on his comprehension of the situation. He pushed back by sharing a special story.

His introduction of a shepherd captured their attention. Each one in the bunch was conscious of the nature of a shepherd's occupation. Sheep are foolish, doltish, and skittish.

They shift position subconsciously. When a delicious section of pasture shows up under the crunching motions of their mouths, some may unintentionally munch their way away from the crush of the sheep population. Or something shiny shimmers and they sashay toward it.

Eventually, comprehension dawns, and they shed the shroud of confusion. Fresh realization of their position shocks them - no other sheep, no shelter, no shepherd as far as their vision shows.

They've been shanghaied by their own shortcomings and can't recall directions back to the sheepfold.

They may shuffle too near the edge of a sheer drop-off and find themselves caught between sharp shards of rock and vexatious shrubs. They are in rough shape and are shaken by their treacherous situation. Are they shivering from the drop in temperature or from their ferocious fear?

The shepherd is conscious of the fact that his count is one short. Only ninety-nine show up as he shoos the sheep toward the shed. One has vanished.

To assure the safety of the larger bunch, the shepherd manufactures a shield of branches and rocks to section them off from the open pasture. Then he sets off on his mission to flush out the location of his missing sheep.

The anxious stray is reassured to hear shouts as the shepherd approaches. Proficient in the use of his shaft, the shepherd unshackles the lamb from his precarious perch. He establishes the shaky one securely on his substantial shoulders.

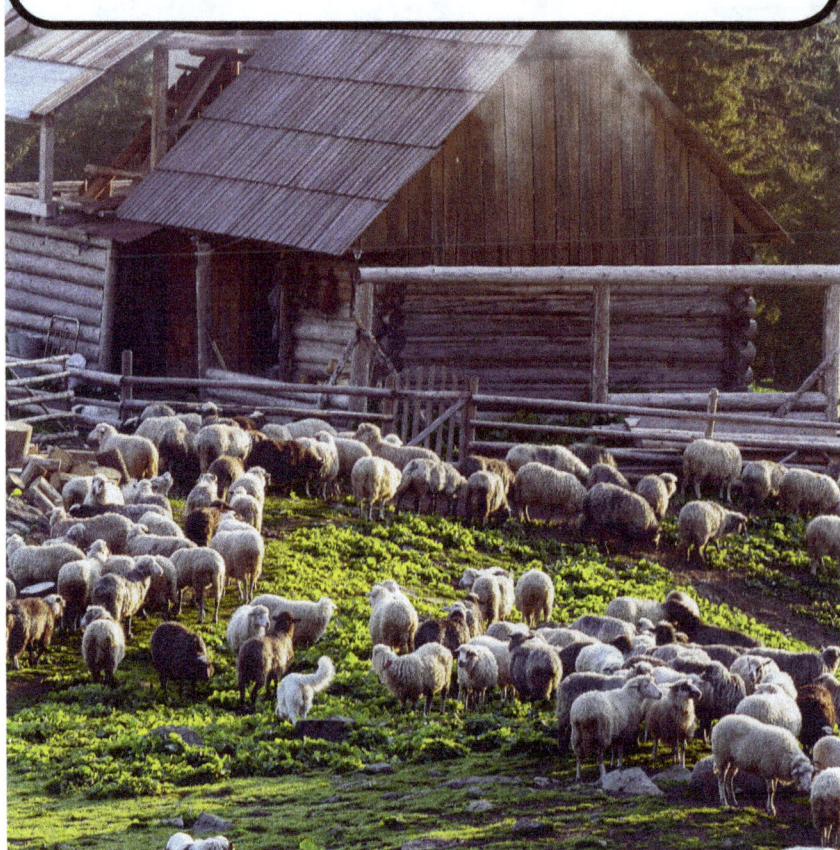

There is no plan for punishment in the shepherd's heart, just an expression of satisfaction and elation. Approaching home, the shepherd's face is awash with emotion. It is surely clear to everyone that he treasures each of his precious sheep and is thrilled to have them all back, sheltered safely under his watchful eye.

In much the same way, there is celebration in heaven when one who has been lost in transgression shows anguish over his sin. His decision to relinquish shame and receive God's gracious gift initiates a worship service among the angels.

The reestablishment of this one heart into the Father's shalom is an even more delicious treasure than the ninety-nine who had never pushed him away.

THE KING'S BANQUET

New ideas:
1.
2.
3.

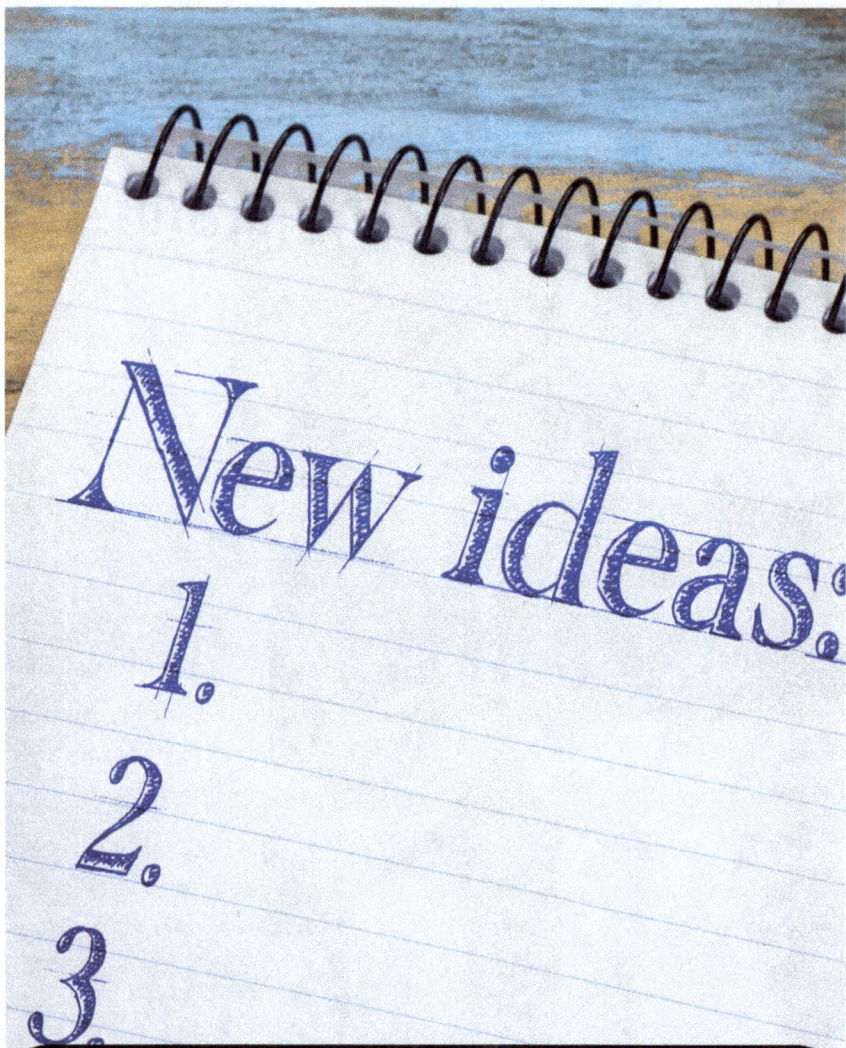

The king was thinking about the folks in his kingdom and conceived of a cool course of action that would encourage them. He could have a carnival, a barbeque, or possibly a banquet. Cost was not a factor. And he could include all as his companions for whatever activity he picked.

He had key members of his cadre work out the particulars. When all the technicalities were completed, he told the crew chief to circulate a squad through the crowd. The workers were to convey the king's request for all to come to his banquet.

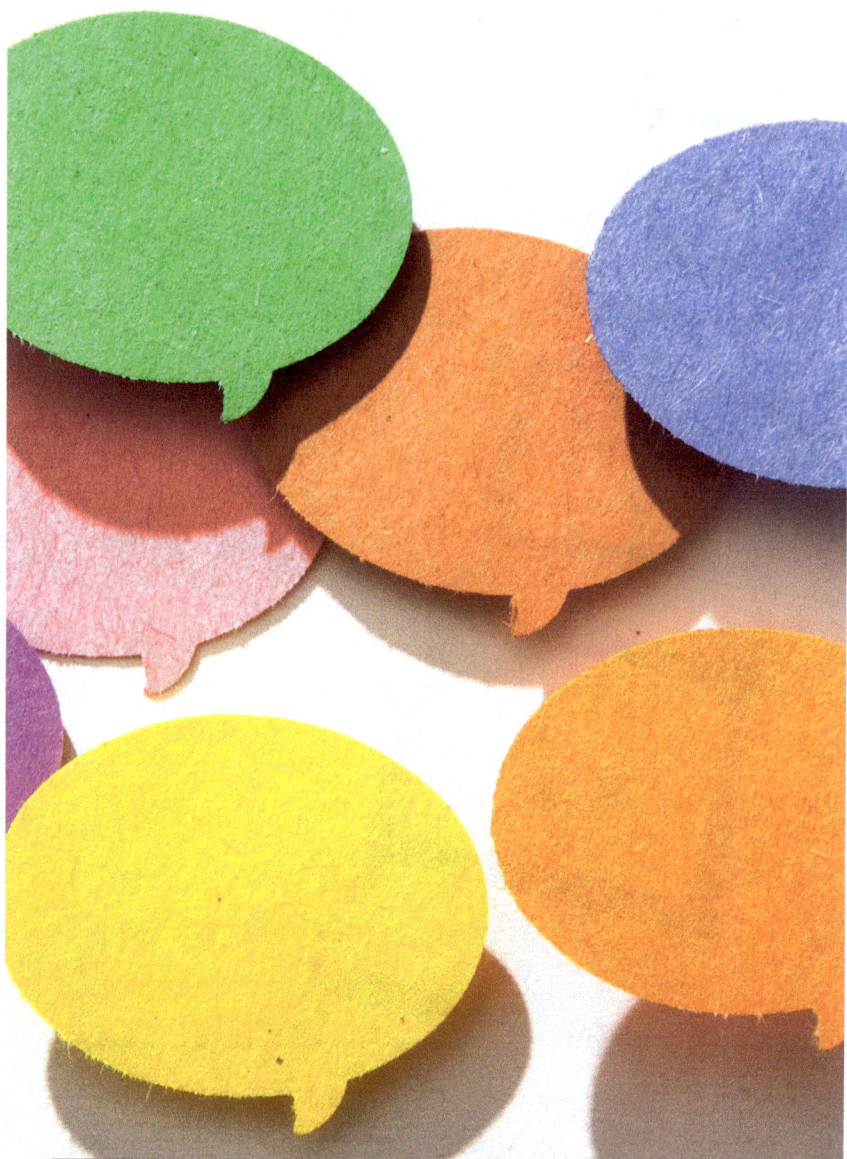

The excuses came quite quickly as scores of folks declined the king's offer.

"I've just become the squire of some new acreage, and I must clock in to inspect it. My company is required. In any case, thanks for thinking of me."

"I have acquired quite a few new cows and am committed to scrutinizing their quality - you can't be too careful when it comes to new cows. Check back with me later."

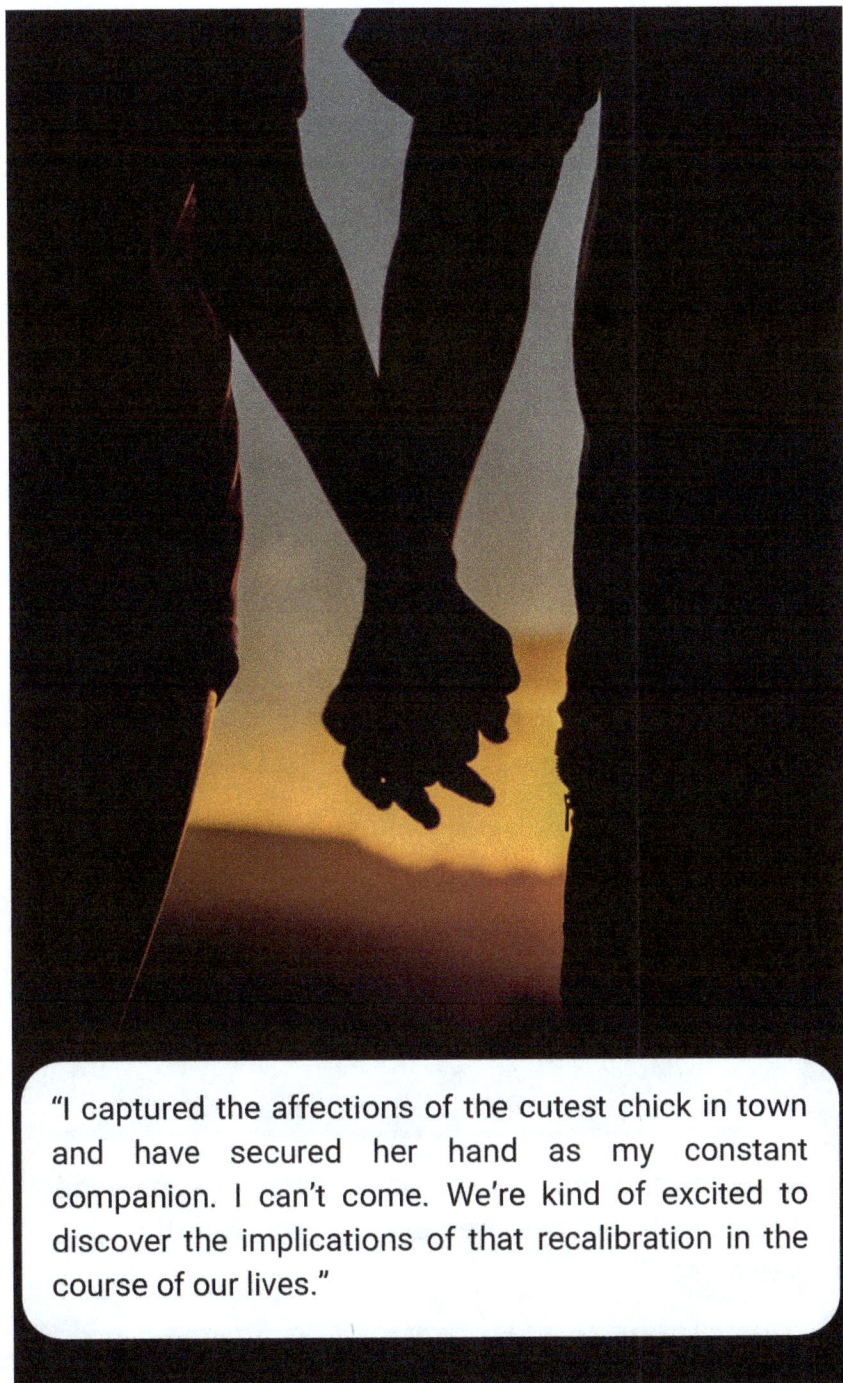

"I captured the affections of the cutest chick in town and have secured her hand as my constant companion. I can't come. We're kind of excited to discover the implications of that recalibration in the course of our lives."

When the crew chief came back to the courtyard and disclosed these comments from the clan, the king was cross.

He commanded the corps to quickly backtrack. This time, they were to concentrate on all the cracks and crevasses where the broken might take cover.

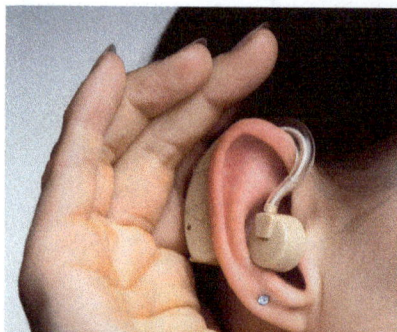

Seek out the handicapped and incapacitated. If they are out of commission, they might be secluded behind a curtain of darkness.

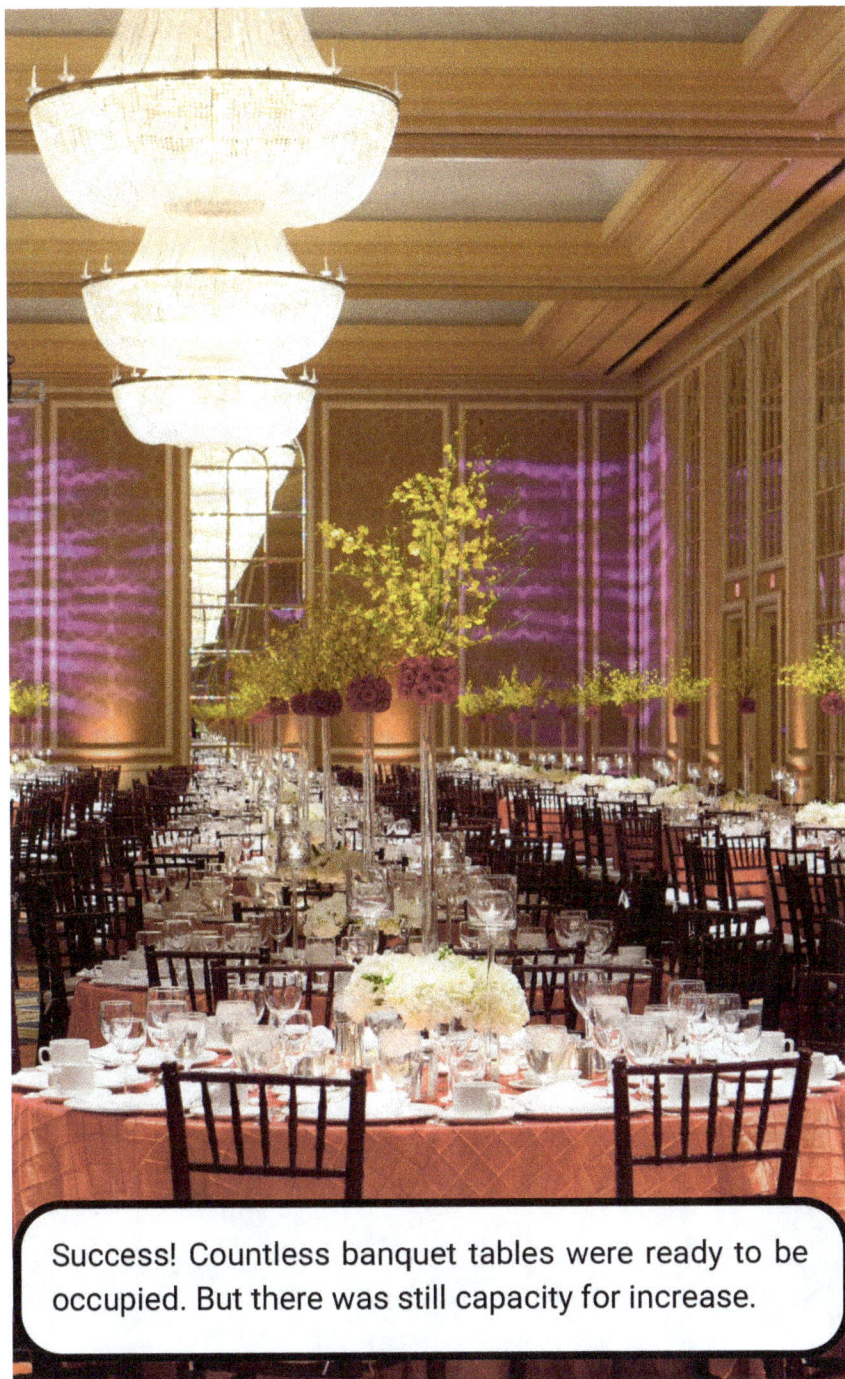

Success! Countless banquet tables were ready to be occupied. But there was still capacity for increase.

The director was instructed to take all the workers and cross over to the next county. Cover as many sectors as they could. Convince all they talked to that they were welcome. Call the public to come whether they lived close by or came in from the outskirts.

"I want this banquet hall crowded! I want it chock-full and packed from corner to corner," was the king's decree.

The king's countenance quieted as he reflected on those in the community who had forsaken his kindness. They would be blocked from collecting even a miniscule scrap of the delicacies conferred upon the folks who came to the king's banquet.

THE WHEAT
AND THE WEEDS

A wealthy squire sowed his field with wonderful wheat seeds. His workers were equipped with the required qualifications to produce a quality crop for the owner. They went about their day in full swing and earned their wages well.

As twilight approached the workers withdrew to their beds. A wicked foe weaseled his way under the wire.

Working in the shadows, he quickly strew unwieldy weeds in with the handiwork that had been woven by the daytime squad. Then he quietly whisked himself away before dawn.

When green wisps of wheat worked their way upward and the grain began to grow, the workmen also witnessed the unwelcome weeds. They went to the owner with this news.

"Your seed was squeaky clean. From where did these weeds ensue? Should we twist them out?"

The owner was wise. He said, "No, if you try to wipe out the weed you will waste some of the wheat. Let them grow as one for now."

One thing that the owner knew was how the two plants would flower. When wheat has quickened and is fully grown, its seeds are weighty. It dips its crown down when blown by the wind as if in worship. But when the weeds are full-grown, they look proud. While they are known to be worthless, they stand unswervingly straight as if to willfully say, "Watch me!"

When the window of waiting passed, the workers, with the help of the wind, were able to winnow the wheat from the weeds with ease.

Be aware of what these words mean:

- The one who sows the seeds is the Son of Man.

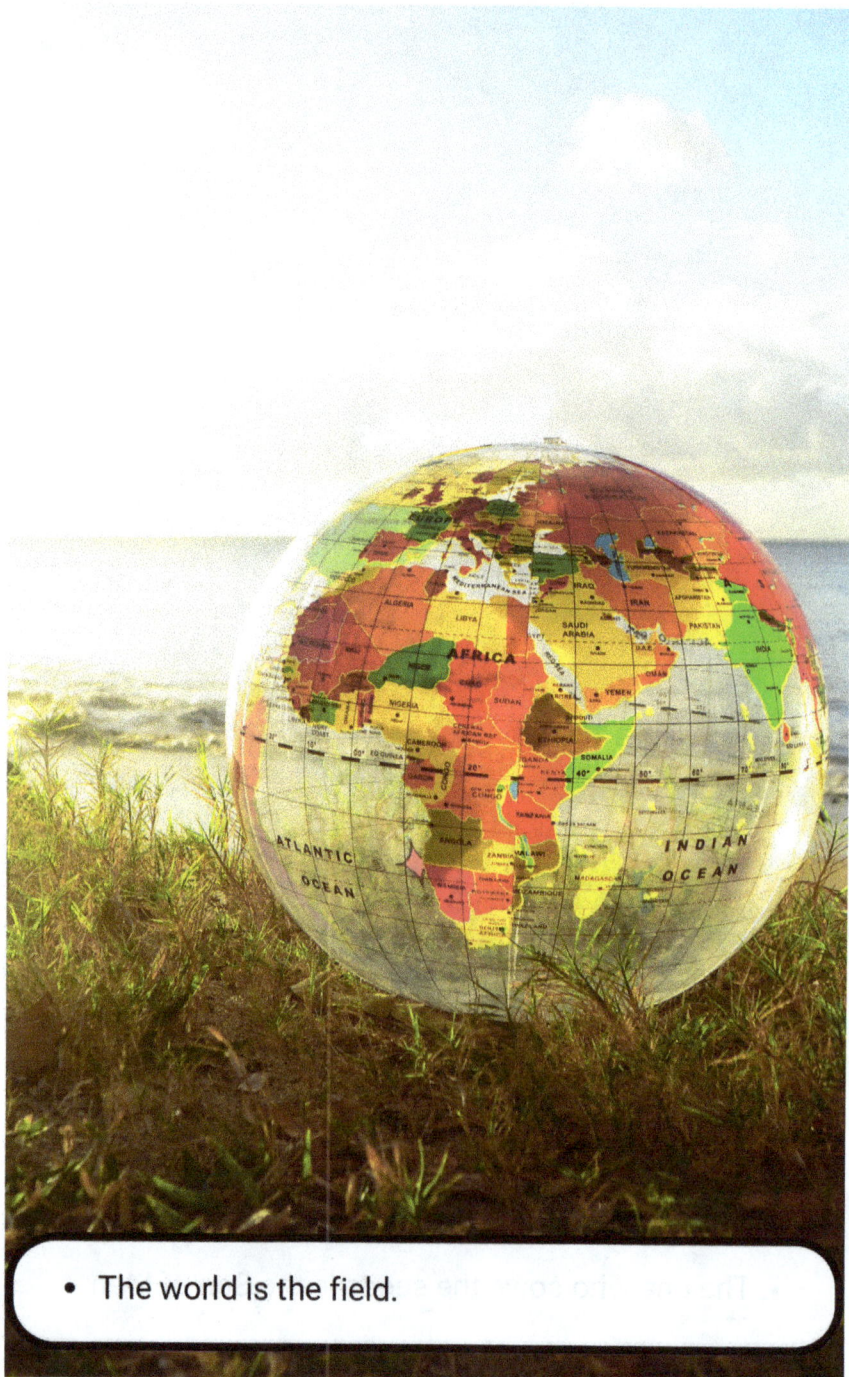

- The world is the field.

- The unwavering ones in the commonwealth of heaven are the wheat seeds.

- The wicked foes who work for the evil one are the weeds.

- The winnowing will happen at the end of the
  world.

- The workers are God's angels.

Be watchful, and grow into ones who would bow as the wheat in worship of their owner. Then you will glow like the sun for all the world to witness.

SMART VERSUS SILLY

So many in society say "Yes" to the Savior but don't understand the seriousness of that promise.

Yes, I will confess my sins unless it embarrasses me to speak of them.

Yes, I will seek your face except when I am so sleepy and need my rest.

Yes, I will stick to your steps unless I find a more interesting solution.

Yes, I will serve others unless I am frustrated with something they say or do.

Yes, I will rejoice in times of sorrow unless it's too hard to trust your strategy.

Yes, I will surrender to your Spirit unless he asks me to do something too toilsome or exhausting.

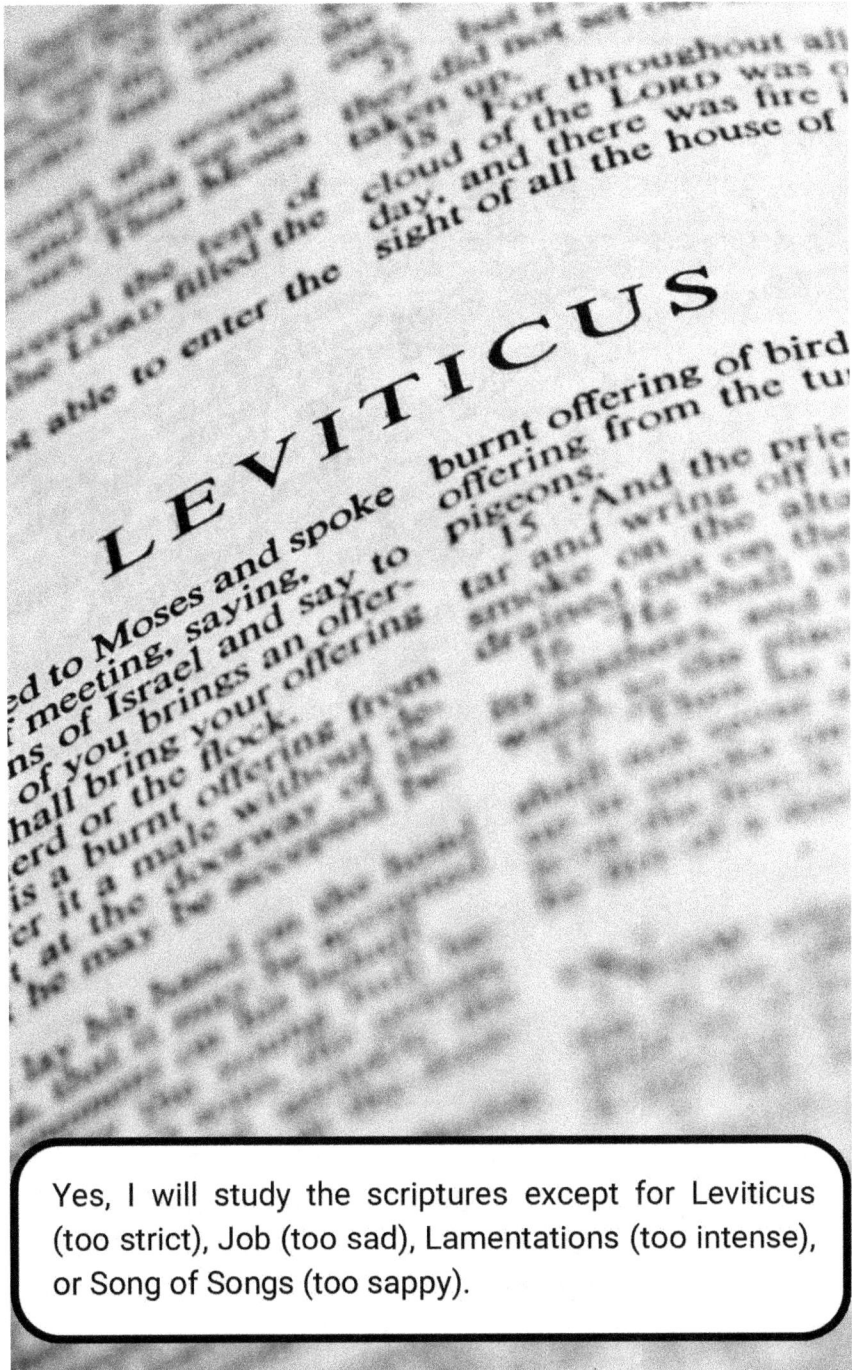

Yes, I will study the scriptures except for Leviticus (too strict), Job (too sad), Lamentations (too intense), or Song of Songs (too sappy).

Jesus had a serious discussion about listening to and obeying his words. The last thing he said in his most famous Sermon went something like this:

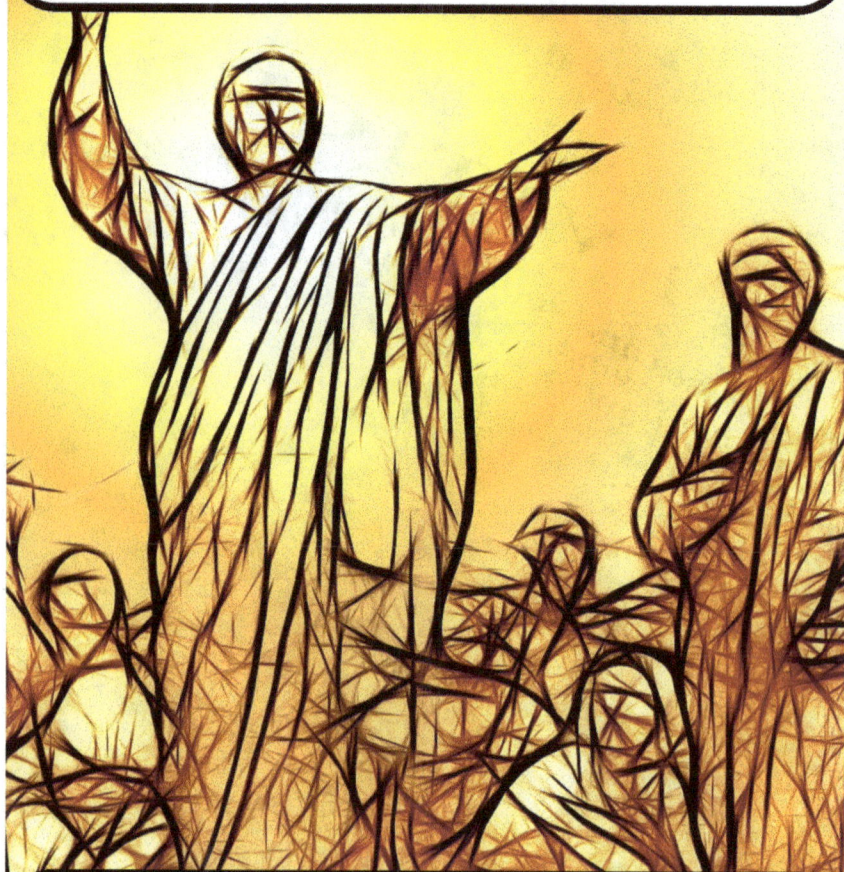

Those who listen to my words and live consistently according to their principles are wise (as in sensible, smart, perceptive, and discerning). See if this image helps you to understand:

A wise person (this is someone who hears my words and does what they say) constructed his house near the sea. He made certain that the substructure was solid. He assembled all the pieces on a strong slab.

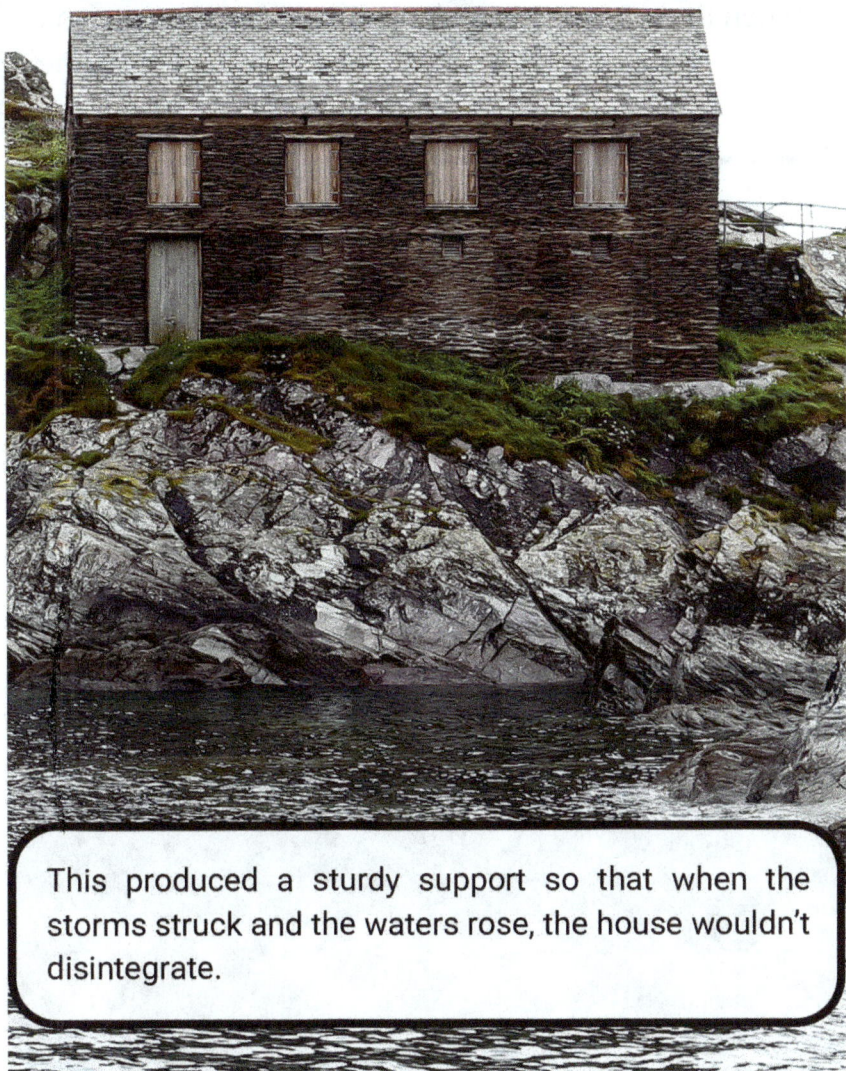

This produced a sturdy support so that when the storms struck and the waters rose, the house wouldn't disintegrate.

An ill-advised and brainless person (this is someone who hears my words but thinks they are stupid and ignores them) also chose to construct his house near the sea. In contrast, he assembled his residence on the sand. This enterprise was much less successful. When the rain and sleet slashed against the walls and the floods surged against the doors and windows, the structure collapsed with a robust blast.

The scores of listeners who sat in circles, concentrating on this extensive sermon, were astounded. Jesus amazed them with the instructions he spoke, for his words were forceful. He had a mastery over the law that their ecclesiastical teachers did not possess.

This is how to respond wisely to Jesus' teachings:

Yes, I will confess my sins, for then you will cast them away as far as the east is from the west.

Yes, I will seek your face, for you are the one who gives me strength to do all things at all times.

Yes, I will stick to your steps, because when I trust in you, you make my paths straight.

Yes, I will serve others and esteem them as I esteem myself.

Yes, I will rejoice in times of sorrow because in you I find peace.

Yes, I will surrender to your Spirit because you establish my way.

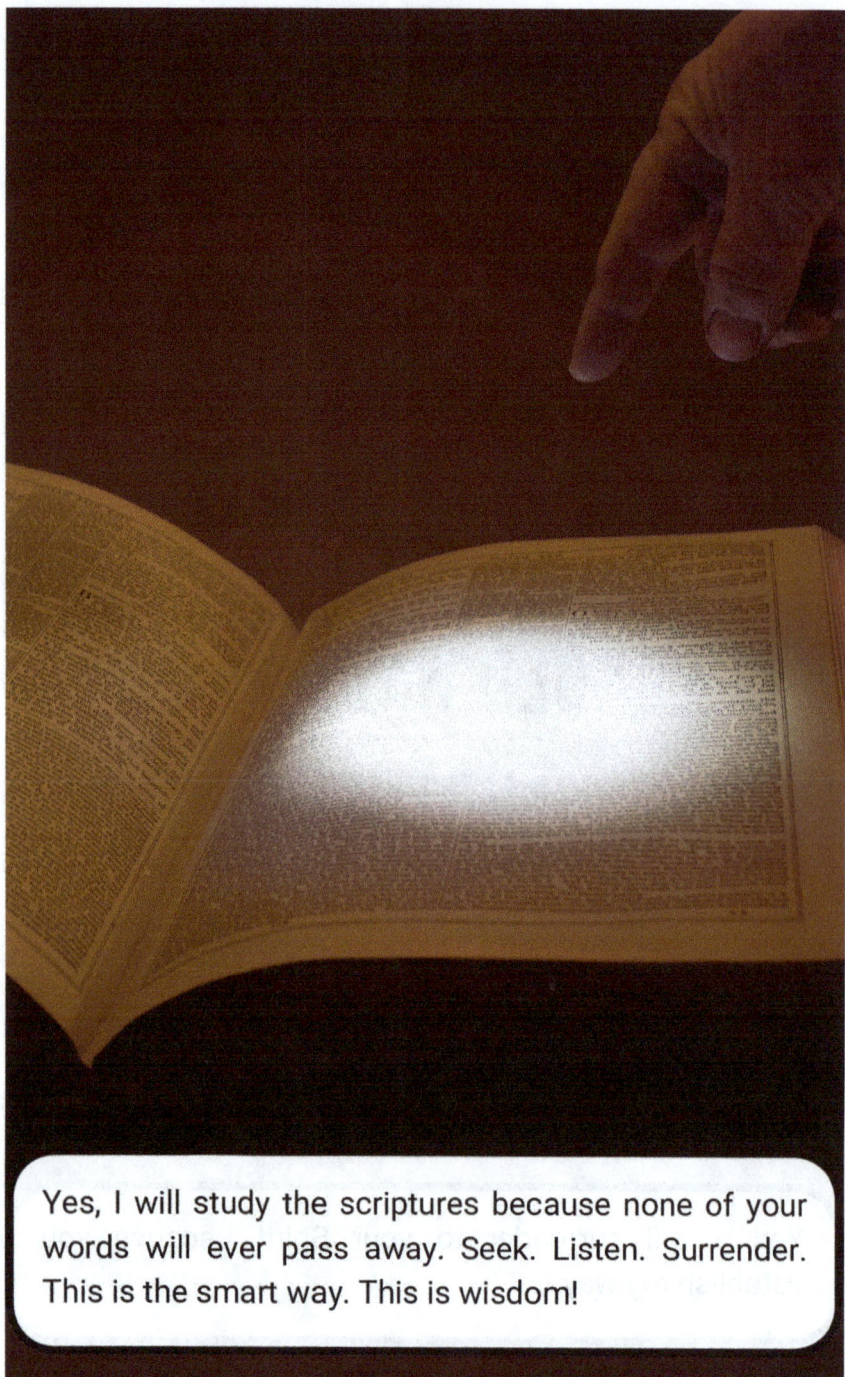

Yes, I will study the scriptures because none of your words will ever pass away. Seek. Listen. Surrender. This is the smart way. This is wisdom!

LOCAL LABORERS MEET LIBERAL LANDLORD

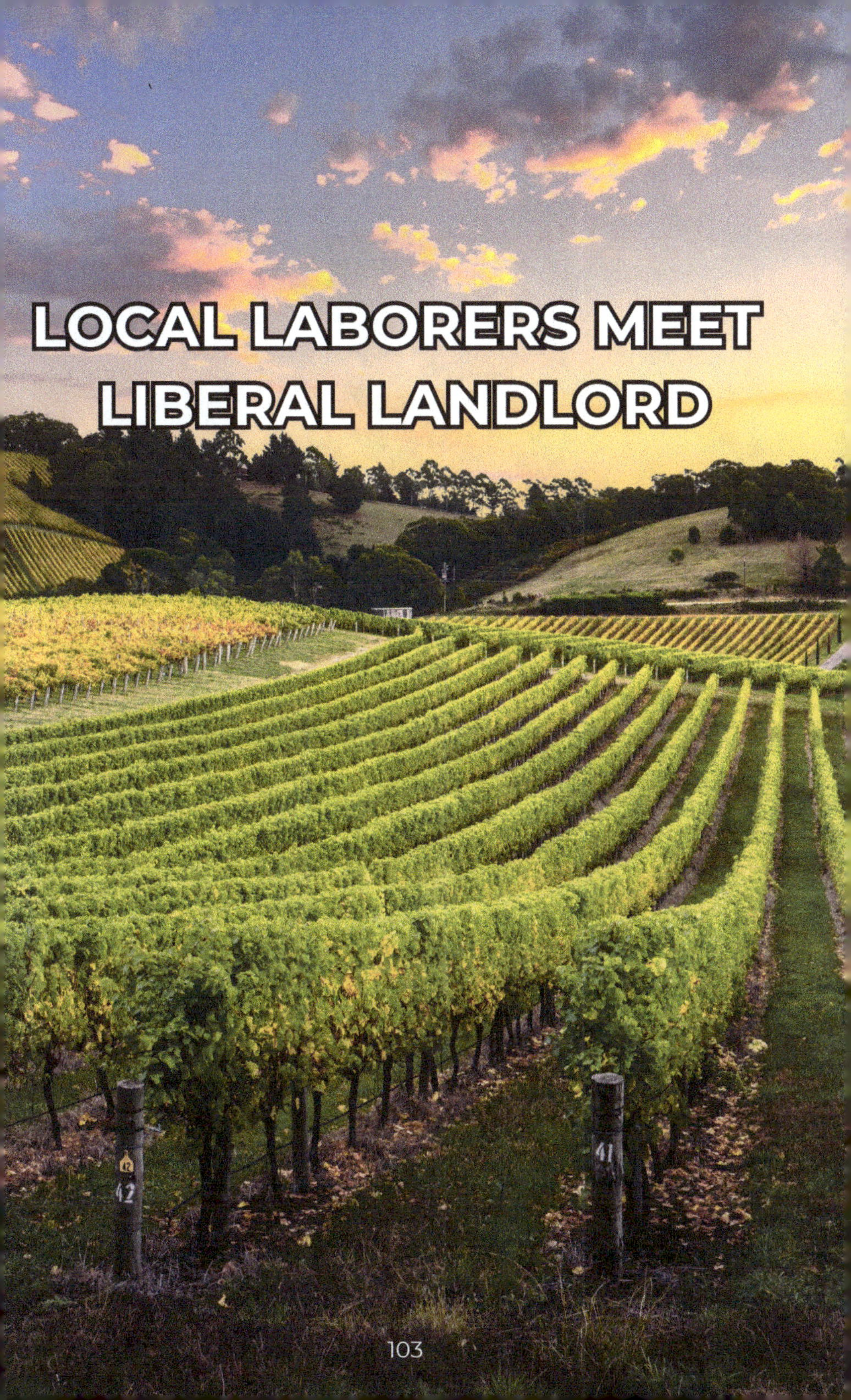

A landowner left home at first light, looking for skilled laborers to till the soil, landscape his fields, and cultivate the flora on his plantation.

Checklist

- ☑
- ☑
- ☑
- ☑
- ☑

He had lots of slots to fill and told them all the level of salary they would collect for their toil.

The lucky hirelings were glad to locate employment and thrilled with the outlay that the landowner had stipulated.

At nine o'clock, the landlord lit upon another platoon of planters who were lazing idly in the hamlet and employed them for the same daily wage. At twelve o'clock and at three o'clock, he did likewise.

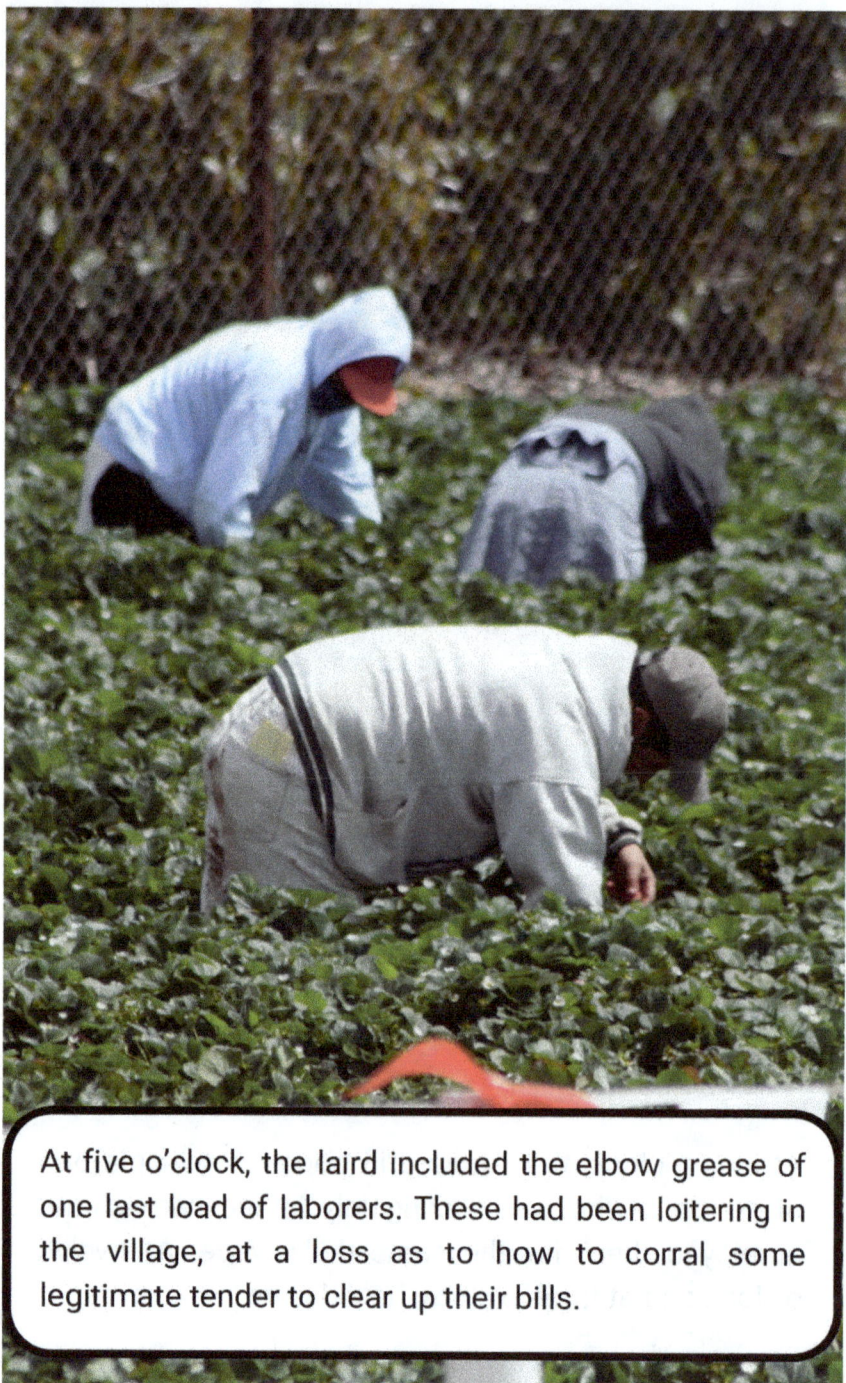

At five o'clock, the laird included the elbow grease of one last load of laborers. These had been loitering in the village, at a loss as to how to corral some legitimate tender to clear up their bills.

Not long after this last load landed, all labor halted. The fields were ill-lit, and lots of the lads were sleepy.

The lead controller called them all to line up. He plunked down the loot on the table that had been laid aside for each lucky fella.

When the latecomers collected the full salary for less labor, the early birds complained loudly.

"Look here! Lots of us worked the land all day long in the sweltering fields. We believe a larger salary belongs to us."

The landowner replied calmly, "There is nothing cruel or unlawful in our deal. When I put out feelers for fellas to labor for a full day on my land, you welcomed the salary. It was legit, and it was plenty."

"Now you are jealous of my liberality toward the lads who worked less time for the same salary. Take your silver and leave. Don't be sullen about my loving outlook on life."

first last

Let it be acknowledged that the early birds will end up last and the last to pull in will relocate to the leading place in line.

TWO MEN
AT THE TEMPLE

The Teacher (capital *T*) might have been invited as a guest to present at a meeting of the Self-Assertive Society.

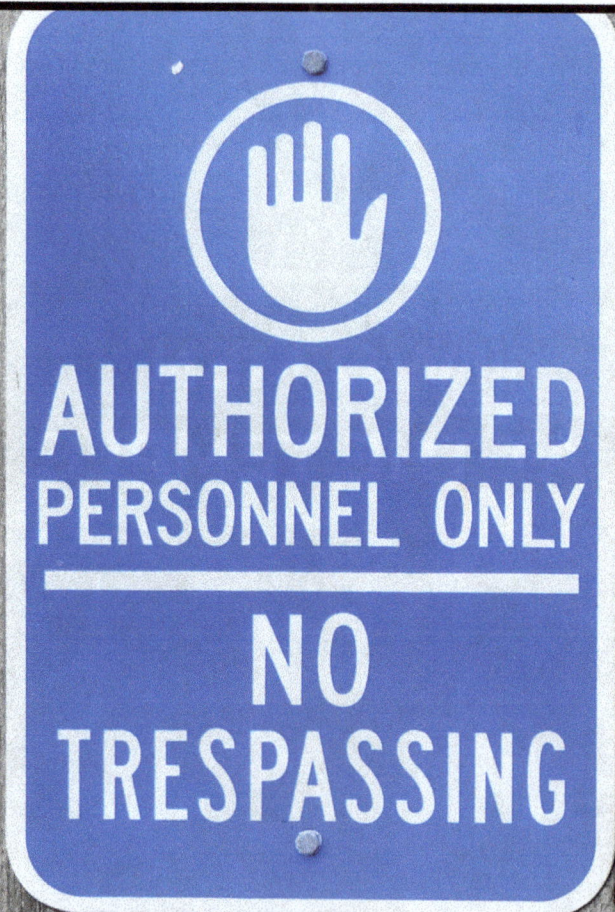

AUTHORIZED PERSONNEL ONLY

NO TRESPASSING

Those who turned out for this particular event (the attendance list was trickled out by a secret spotter) were known to have certifiable narcissistic tendencies.

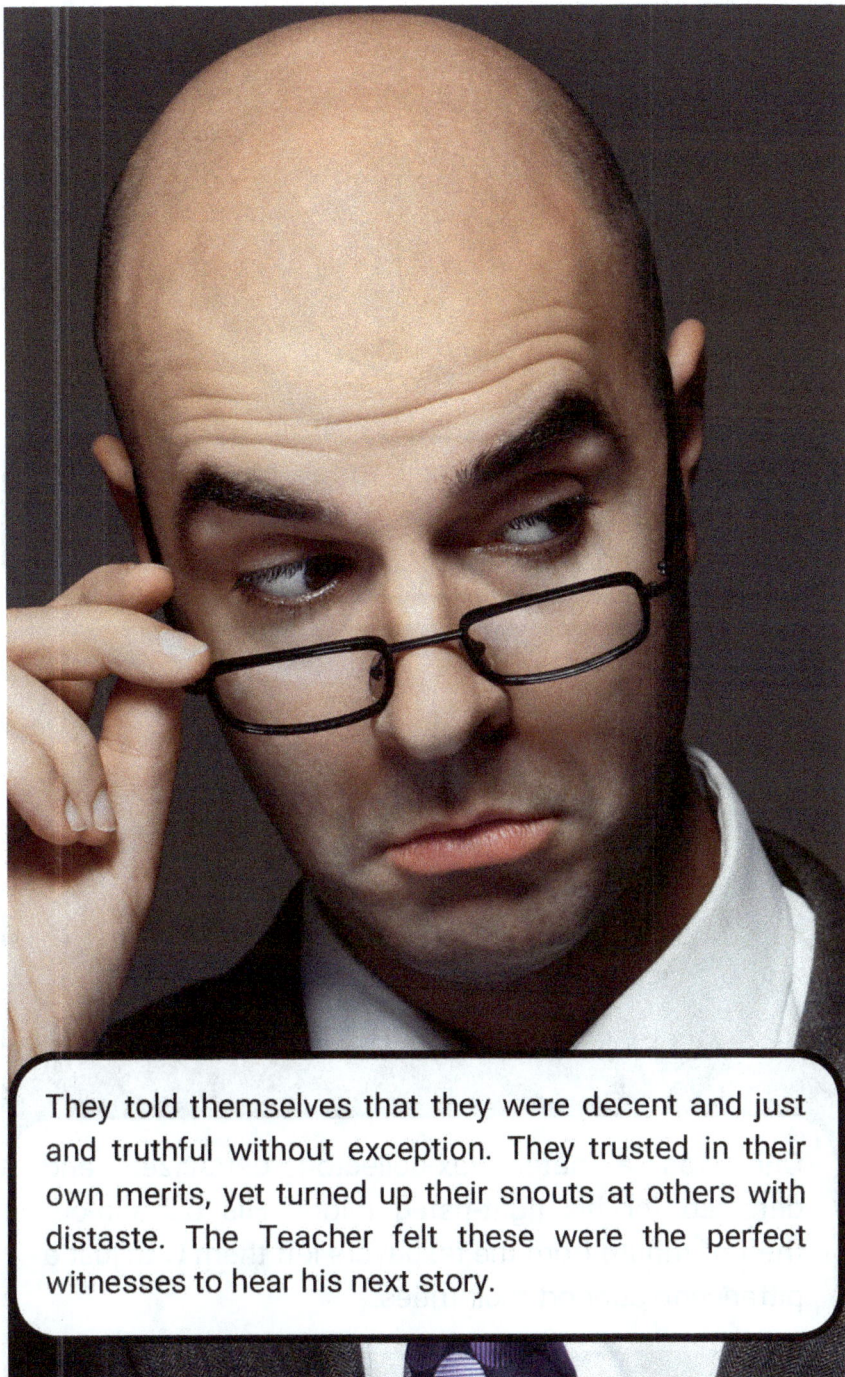

They told themselves that they were decent and just and truthful without exception. They trusted in their own merits, yet turned up their snouts at others with distaste. The Teacher felt these were the perfect witnesses to hear his next story.

Two men went to the temple to talk to Almighty God. One was a teacher in the temple - distinguished, esteemed, and important.

One was a hated tax-collector, ostracized and detested for his tight-fisted might. His out-and-out theft of tribute from the taxpayers left them with just a pittance to support their tribes.

The teacher (lowercase *t*) attempted to intimate that he was upright and devout. Truth be told, he strutted to the center stage and started to tastelessly and blatantly list his attributes. He gloated internally, noticing that everyone in the temple was paying attention.

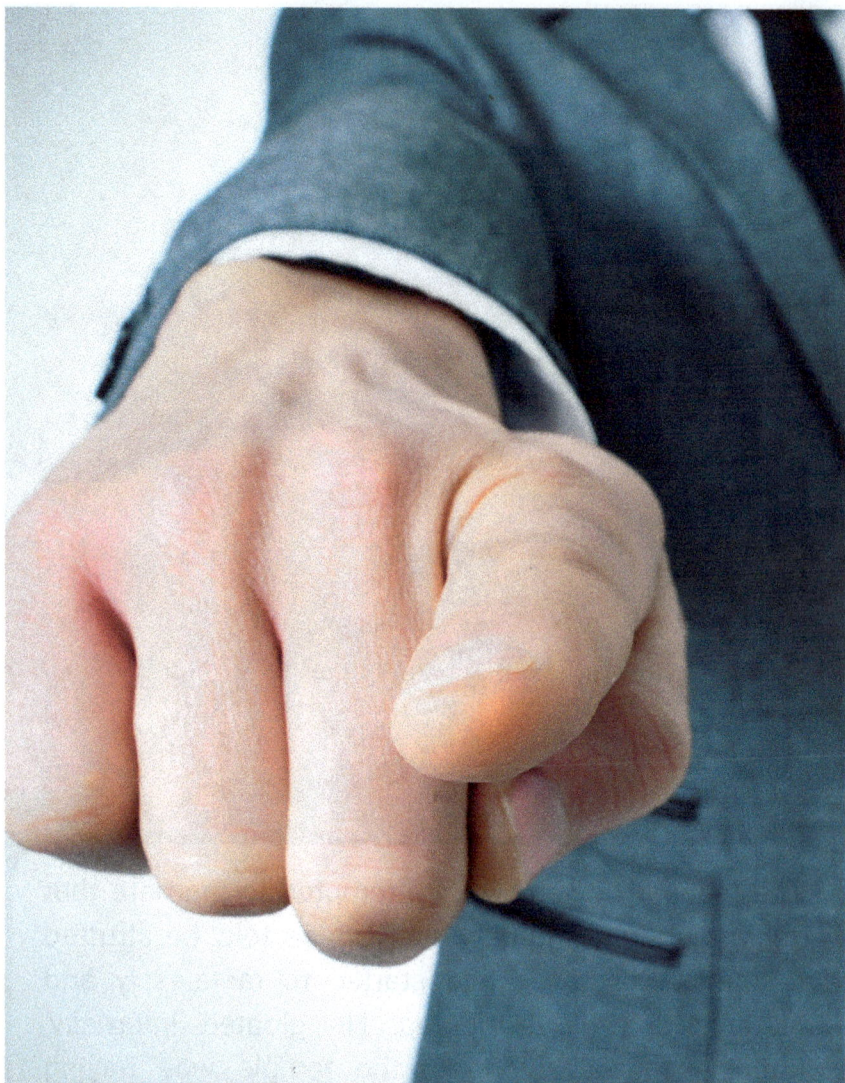

"I'm grateful, Master, to point out that I am not terrible, and I am not a trickster. Mostly, I am not trash like that tax collector trying to hide next to the post over there.

"The entire town can testify that I don't cheat, and I don't take liberties where I shouldn't.

"On top of all of that, I fast two times a week. And I donate a tenth of my treasure to the tabernacle's repository. Quite a lot of boasting points, but I'm not one to elevate myself."

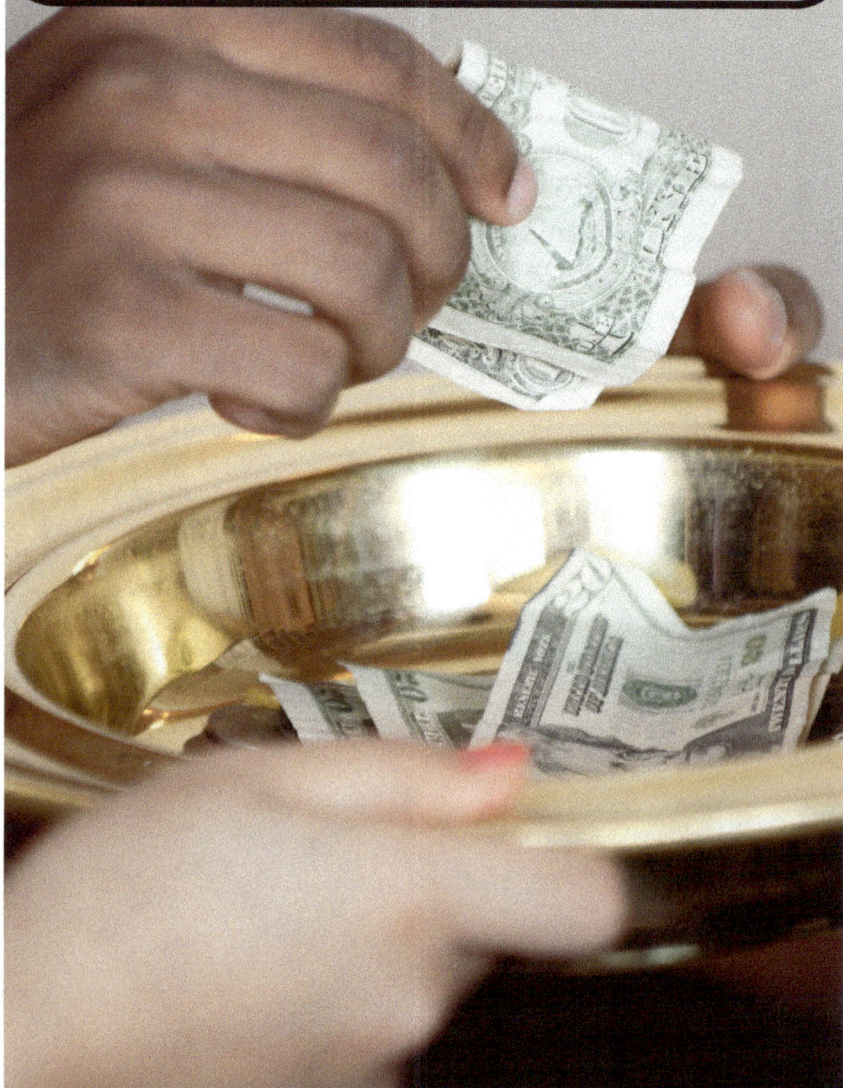

The tax collector stood apart, trembling with the strain of his betrayal. He was timid and hesitant to tarry in the habitation of the Mighty One. He wilted under the weight of his transgressions. His features were contorted with guilt.

"How can you forget my terrible conduct and my heartless actions toward the multitudes? I've brought hurt and distress to all I touched. I have no right to stand here and request tolerance, let alone tenderness. Take pity on me."

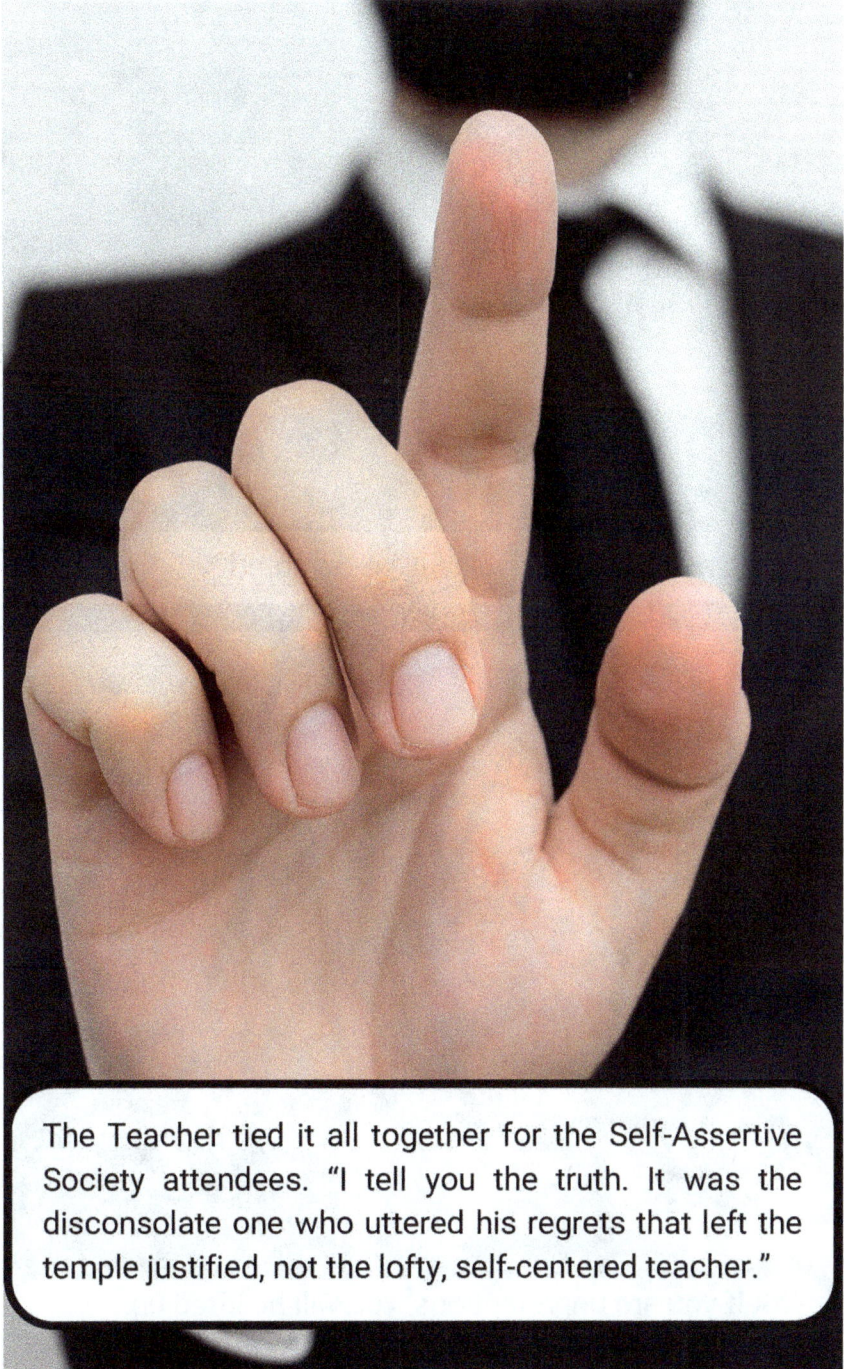

The Teacher tied it all together for the Self-Assertive Society attendees. "I tell you the truth. It was the disconsolate one who uttered his regrets that left the temple justified, not the lofty, self-centered teacher."

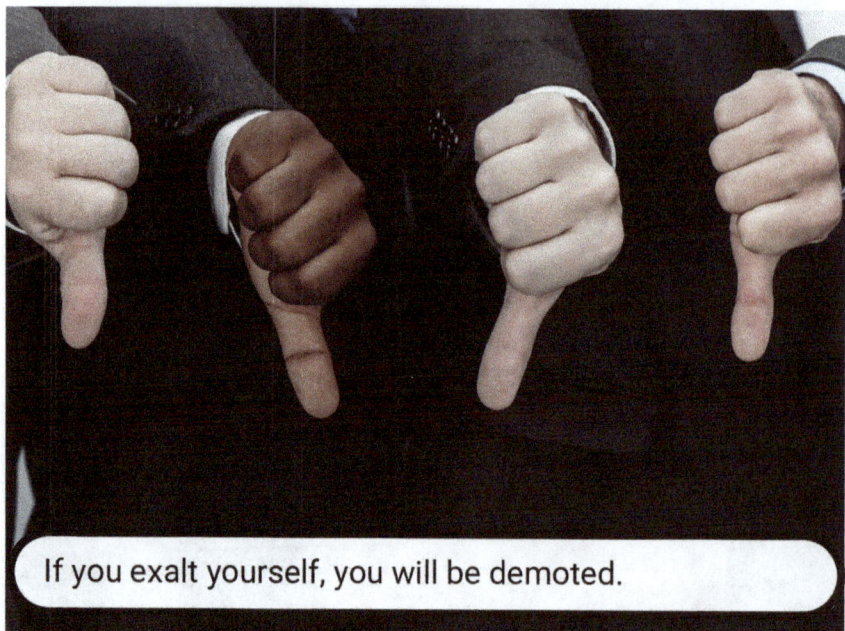

If you exalt yourself, you will be demoted.

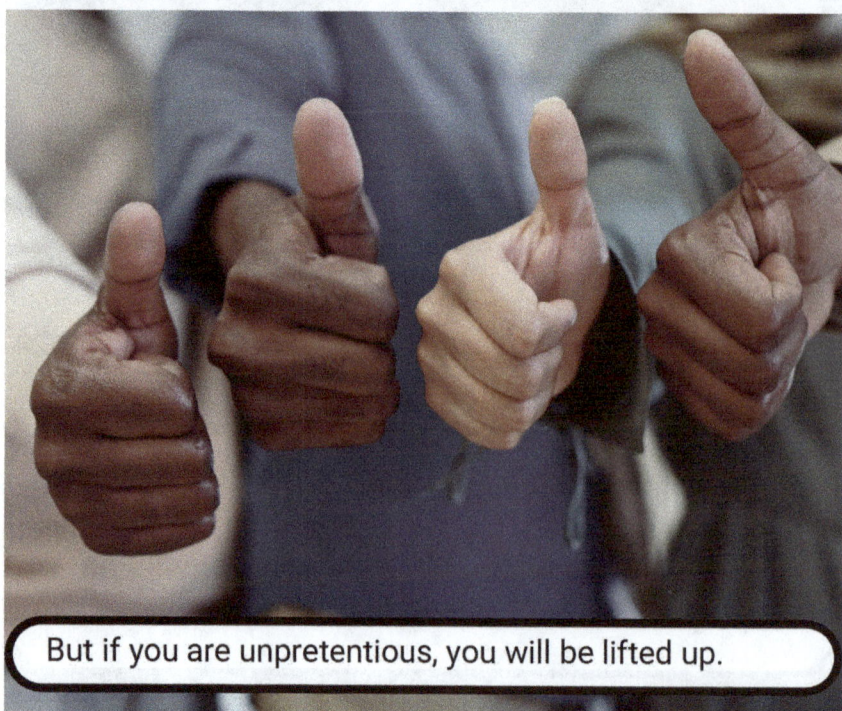

But if you are unpretentious, you will be lifted up.

FINDING FAVOR WITH A FRIEND

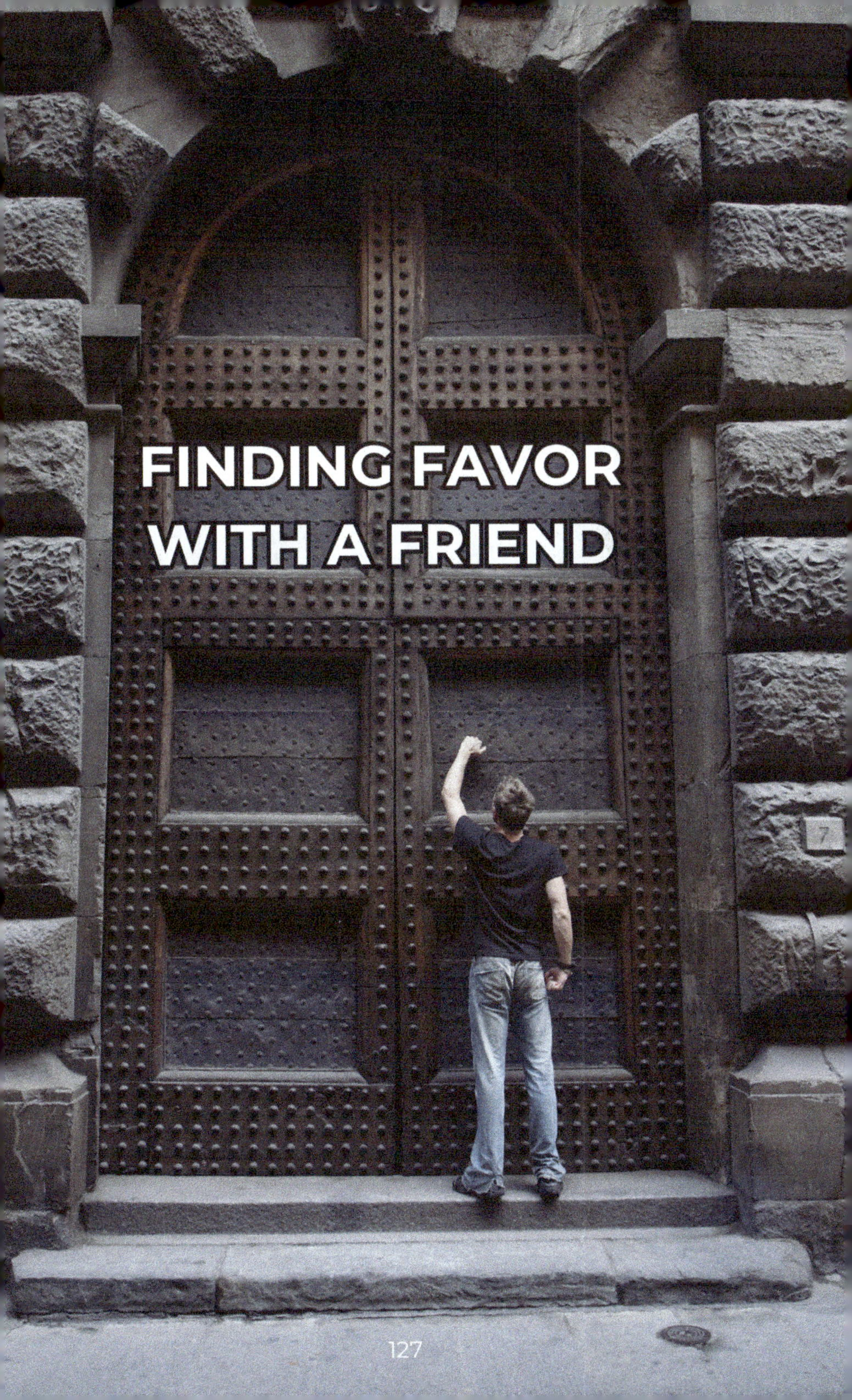

When Jesus finished fellowshipping with his Father, one of the folks who followed after him asked, "Inform us how to confer with the Father as you do." Jesus said, "Hold fast to this kind of format."

Father, you fill the atmosphere. Your fame is forever.

Fix this sphere by filling it with your infinite fullness.

Feed us. Forgive us. Form forgiveness inside of us.

Be a safe refuge for us, and make us steadfast and faithful to follow after you.

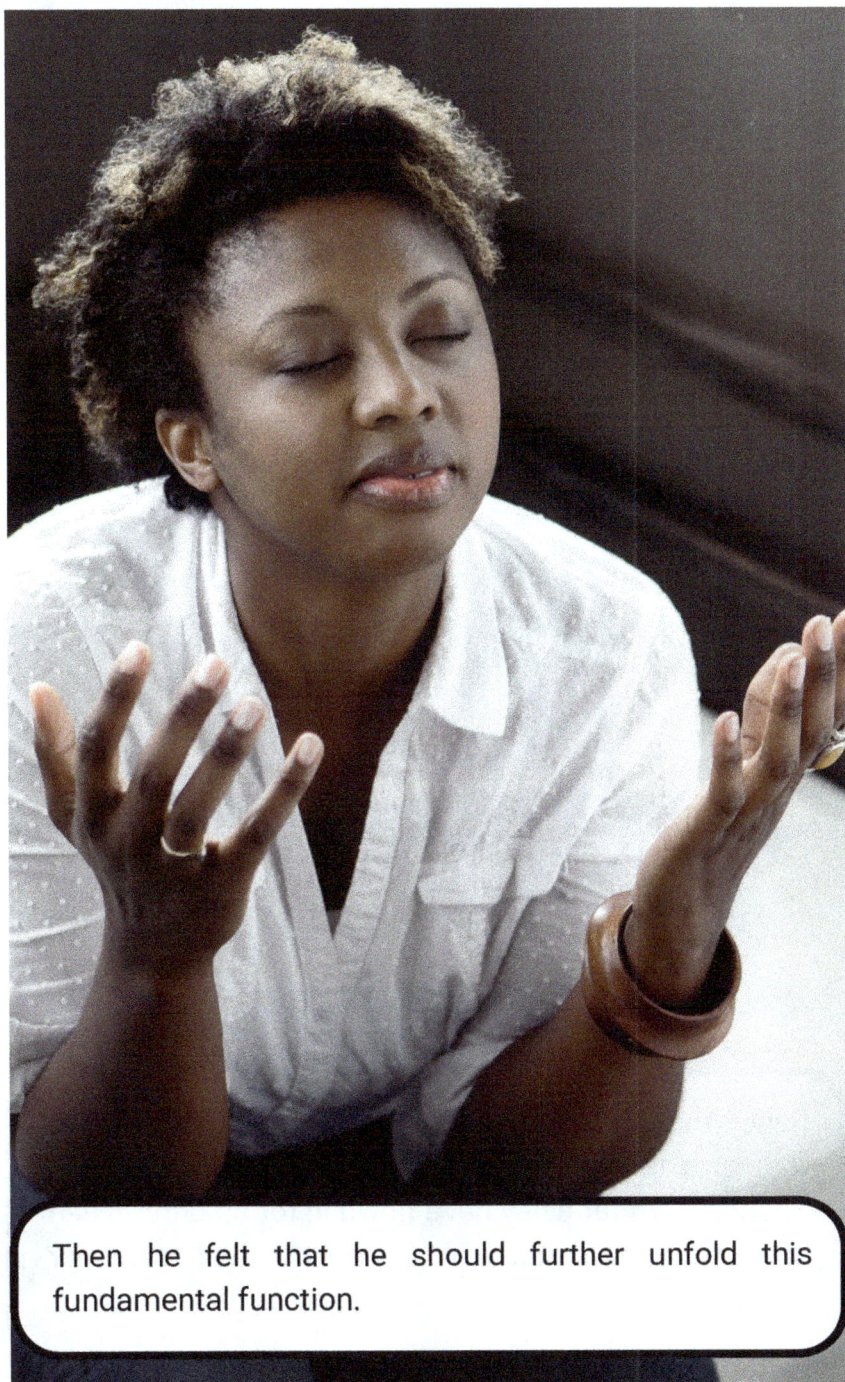

Then he felt that he should further unfold this fundamental function.

Fancy this: You find yourself in front of your friend's flat far after it's fair to find him in a wakeful state. Friends from far away have flown in for an unforeseen stop-off at your place. You have no food to fix for them.

Your fist finds the door, and you buffet it until your sleepy friend is forced to afford feedback.

"My family and I have flaked out for the night. We're getting our forty winks, and we have no food to furnish you. Find your way back home and forget it!"

But you stand firm. You refuse to forsake your formidable refrain. Defeat is not your preference. You must have food.

You flatter. You fawn. You beg and plead for favor. You tough it out until he finally folds. He flings himself from his feather bed, fumbles his way to his foodstuffs, and furnishes you with the fare you need to forego your friends' famishment.

Don't forget these four features when you pray:
- Be unflagging.
- Ask frequently.
- Seek fervently.
- Knock firmly.

Here's the payoff:

- If you ask, it is transferred to you.
- If you seek, you will find.
- If you knock, the way will be free and clear.

SCRIPTURE REFERENCES FROM THE NEW LIVING TRANSLATION:

1. A PARABLE OF THE PLANTS:
PATTERNED AFTER THIS PARABLE SPOKEN BY JESUS IN MATTHEW 13:3-9, 18-23

"Listen! A farmer went out to plant some seeds. As he scattered them across his field, some seeds fell on a footpath, and the birds came and ate them. Other seeds fell on shallow soil with underlying rock. The seeds sprouted quickly because the soil was shallow. But the plants soon wilted under the hot sun, and since they didn't have deep roots, they died. Other seeds fell among thorns that grew up and choked out the tender plants. Still other seeds fell on fertile soil, and they produced a crop that was thirty, sixty, and even a hundred times as much as had been planted! Anyone with ears to hear should listen and understand."

"Now listen to the explanation of the parable about the farmer planting seeds: The seed that fell on the footpath represents those who hear the message about the Kingdom and don't understand it. Then the evil one comes and snatches away the seed that was planted in their hearts. The seed on the rocky soil represents those who hear the message and immediately receive it with joy. But since they don't have deep roots, they don't last long. They fall away as soon as they have problems or are persecuted for believing God's word. The seed that fell among the thorns represents those who hear God's word, but all too quickly the message is crowded out by the worries of this life and the lure of wealth, so no fruit is produced. The seed that fell on good soil represents those who truly hear and understand God's word and produce a harvest of thirty, sixty, or even a hundred times as much as had been planted!"

2. THE SON WHO STRAYED:
PATTERNED AFTER THE PARABLE OF THE PRODIGAL SON SPOKEN BY JESUS IN LUKE 15:11-32

"A man had two sons. The younger son told his father, 'I want my share of your estate now before you die.' So his father agreed to divide his wealth between his sons.

"A few days later this younger son packed all his belongings and moved to a distant land, and there he wasted all his money in wild living. About the time his money ran out, a great famine swept over the land, and he began to starve. He persuaded a local farmer to hire him, and the man sent him into his fields to feed the pigs. The young man became so hungry that even the pods he was feeding the pigs looked good to him. But no one gave him anything.

"When he finally came to his senses, he said to himself, 'At home even the hired servants have food enough to spare, and here I am dying of hunger! I will go home to my father and say, "Father, I have sinned against both heaven and you, and I am no longer worthy of being called your son. Please take me on as a hired servant."'

"So he returned home to his father. And while he was still a long way off, his father saw him coming. Filled with love and compassion, he ran to his son, embraced him, and kissed him. His son said to him, 'Father, I have sinned against both heaven and you, and I am no longer worthy of being called your son.'

"But his father said to the servants, 'Quick! Bring the finest robe in the house and put it on him. Get a ring for his finger and sandals for his feet. And kill the calf we have been fattening. We must celebrate with a feast, for this son of mine was dead and has now returned to life. He was lost, but now he is found.' So the party began.

"Meanwhile, the older son was in the fields working. When he returned home, he heard music and dancing in the house, and he asked one of the servants what was going on. 'Your brother is back,' he was told, 'and your father has killed the fattened calf. We are celebrating because of his safe return.'

"The older brother was angry and wouldn't go in. His father came out and begged him, but he replied, 'All these years I've slaved for you and never once refused to do a single thing you told me to. And in all that time you never gave me even one young goat for a feast with my friends. Yet when this son of yours comes back after squandering your money on prostitutes, you celebrate by killing the fattened calf!'

"His father said to him, 'Look, dear son, you have always stayed by me, and everything I have is yours. We had to celebrate this happy day. For your brother was dead and has come back to life! He was lost, but now he is found!'"

3. THE LAW LOOKS AT LOVE AND LIFE:
PATTERNED AFTER THE PARABLE OF THE GOOD SAMARITAN SPOKEN BY JESUS IN LUKE 10:25-37

One day an expert in religious law stood up to test Jesus by asking him this question: "Teacher, what should I do to inherit eternal life?"

Jesus replied, "What does the law of Moses say? How do you read it?"

The man answered, "'You must love the Lord your God with all your heart, all your soul, all your strength, and all your mind.' And, 'Love your neighbor as yourself.'"

"Right!" Jesus told him. "Do this and you will live!"

The man wanted to justify his actions, so he asked Jesus, "And who is my neighbor?"

Jesus replied with a story: "A Jewish man was traveling from Jerusalem down to Jericho, and he was attacked by bandits. They stripped him of his clothes, beat him up, and left him half dead beside the road.

"By chance a priest came along. But when he saw the man lying there, he crossed to the other side of the road and passed him by. A Temple assistant walked over and looked at him lying there, but he also passed by on the other side.

"Then a despised Samaritan came along, and when he saw the man, he felt compassion for him. Going over to him, the Samaritan soothed his wounds with olive oil and wine and bandaged them.

Then he put the man on his own donkey and took him to an inn, where he took care of him. The next day he handed the innkeeper two silver coins, telling him, 'Take care of this man. If his bill runs higher than this, I'll pay you the next time I'm here.'

"Now which of these three would you say was a neighbor to the man who was attacked by bandits?" Jesus asked.

The man replied, "The one who showed him mercy.

Then Jesus said, "Yes, now go and do the same."

4. THE SHEPHERD AND THE SHEEP:
PATTERNED AFTER THE PARABLE OF THE LOST SHEEP SPOKEN BY JESUS IN LUKE 15:1-7

Tax collectors and other notorious sinners often came to listen to Jesus teach. This made the Pharisees and teachers of religious law complain that he was associating with such sinful people—even eating with them!

So Jesus told them this story: "If a man has a hundred sheep and one of them gets lost, what will he do? Won't he leave the ninety-nine others in the wilderness and go to search for the one that is lost until he finds it?

And when he has found it, he will joyfully carry it home on his shoulders. When he arrives, he will call together his friends and neighbors, saying, 'Rejoice with me because I have found my lost sheep.'

In the same way, there is more joy in heaven over one lost sinner who repents and returns to God than over ninety-nine others who are righteous and haven't strayed away!

5. THE KING'S BANQUET:
PATTERNED AFTER THE PARABLE OF THE GREAT BANQUET SPOKEN BY JESUS IN LUKE 14:16-24

"A man prepared a great feast and sent out many invitations. When the banquet was ready, he sent his servant to tell the guests, 'Come, the banquet is ready.' But they all began making excuses.

One said, 'I have just bought a field and must inspect it. Please excuse me.' Another said, 'I have just bought five pairs of oxen, and I want to try them out. Please excuse me.' Another said, 'I just got married, so I can't come.'

"The servant returned and told his master what they had said. His master was furious and said, 'Go quickly into the streets and alleys of the town and invite the poor, the crippled, the blind, and the lame.' After the servant had done this, he reported, 'There is still room for more.' So his master said, 'Go out into the country lanes and behind the hedges and urge anyone you find to come, so that the house will be full. For none of those I first invited will get even the smallest taste of my banquet.'"

6. THE WHEAT AND THE WEEDS:
PATTERNED AFTER THE PARABLE SPOKEN BY JESUS IN MATTHEW 13:24-30, 36-43

Here is another story Jesus told: "The Kingdom of Heaven is like a farmer who planted good seed in his field. But that night as the workers slept, his enemy came and planted weeds among the wheat, then slipped away. When the crop began to grow and produce grain, the weeds also grew.

"The farmer's workers went to him and said, 'Sir, the field where you planted that good seed is full of weeds! Where did they come from?'

"'An enemy has done this!' the farmer exclaimed.

"'Should we pull out the weeds?' they asked.

"'No,' he replied, 'you'll uproot the wheat if you do. Let both grow together until the harvest. Then I will tell the harvesters to sort out the weeds, tie them into bundles, and burn them, and to put the wheat in the barn.'"

Then, leaving the crowds outside, Jesus went into the house. His disciples said, "Please explain to us the story of the weeds in the field."

Jesus replied, "The Son of Man is the farmer who plants the good seed. The field is the world, and the good seed represents the people of the Kingdom.

The weeds are the people who belong to the evil one. The enemy who planted the weeds among the wheat is the devil. The harvest is the end of the world, and the harvesters are the angels.

"Just as the weeds are sorted out and burned in the fire, so it will be at the end of the world. The Son of Man will send his angels, and they will remove from his Kingdom everything that causes sin and all who do evil. And the angels will throw them into the fiery furnace, where there will be weeping and gnashing of teeth. Then the righteous will shine like the sun in their Father's Kingdom. Anyone with ears to hear should listen and understand!"

7. SMART VERSUS SILLY:
PATTERNED AFTER THE PARABLE OF THE WISE AND FOOLISH BUILDERS SPOKEN BY JESUS IN MATTHEW 7:24-29

"Anyone who listens to my teaching and follows it is wise, like a person who builds a house on solid rock. Though the rain comes in torrents and the floodwaters rise and the winds beat against that house, it won't collapse because it is built on bedrock. But anyone who hears my teaching and doesn't obey it is foolish, like a person who builds a house on sand. When the rains and floods come and the winds beat against that house, it will collapse with a mighty crash."

When Jesus had finished saying these things, the crowds were amazed at his teaching, for he taught with real authority—quite unlike their teachers of religious law.

8. LOCAL LABORERS MEET LIBERAL LANDOWNER:
PATTERNED AFTER THE PARABLE OF THE VINEYARD SPOKEN BY JESUS IN MATTHEW 20:1-16

"For the Kingdom of Heaven is like the landowner who went out early one morning to hire workers for his vineyard. He agreed to pay the normal daily wage and sent them out to work.

"At nine o'clock in the morning he was passing through the marketplace and saw some people standing around doing nothing. So he hired them, telling them he would pay them whatever was right at the end of the day. So they went to work in the vineyard. At noon and again at three o'clock he did the same thing.

"At five o'clock that afternoon he was in town again and saw some more people standing around. He asked them, 'Why haven't you been working today?'

"They replied, 'Because no one hired us.'

"The landowner told them, 'Then go out and join the others in my vineyard.'

"That evening he told the foreman to call the workers in and pay them, beginning with the last workers first. When those hired at five o'clock were paid, each received a full day's wage. When those hired first came to get their pay, they assumed they would receive more. But they, too, were paid a day's wage.

When they received their pay, they protested to the owner, 'Those people worked only one hour, and yet you've paid them just as much as you paid us who worked all day in the scorching heat.'

"He answered one of them, 'Friend, I haven't been unfair! Didn't you agree to work all day for the usual wage? Take your money and go. I wanted to pay this last worker the same as you. Is it against the law for me to do what I want with my money? Should you be jealous because I am kind to others?'

"So those who are last now will be first then, and those who are first will be last."

9. TWO MEN AT THE TEMPLE:
PATTERNED AFTER THE PARABLE OF THE PHARISEE AND THE TAX COLLECTOR SPOKEN BY JESUS IN LUKE 18:9-14

Then Jesus told this story to some who had great confidence in their own righteousness and scorned everyone else: "Two men went to the Temple to pray. One was a Pharisee, and the other was a despised tax collector. The Pharisee stood by himself and prayed this prayer: 'I thank you, God, that I am not like other people—

cheaters, sinners, adulterers. I'm certainly not like that tax collector! I fast twice a week, and I give you a tenth of my income.'

"But the tax collector stood at a distance and dared not even lift his eyes to heaven as he prayed. Instead, he beat his chest in sorrow, saying, 'O God, be merciful to me, for I am a sinner.' I tell you, this sinner, not the Pharisee, returned home justified before God. For those who exalt themselves will be humbled, and those who humble themselves will be exalted."

10. FINDING FAVOR WITH A FRIEND
PATTERNED AFTER THE PARABLE OF THE FRIEND AT MIDNIGHT SPOKEN BY JESUS IN LUKE 11:1-10

Once Jesus was in a certain place praying. As he finished, one of his disciples came to him and said, "Lord, teach us to pray, just as John taught his disciples."

Jesus said, "This is how you should pray:

"Father, may your name be kept holy.

May your Kingdom come soon.

Give us each day the food we need,

and forgive us our sins, as we forgive those who sin against us.

And don't let us yield to temptation."

Then, teaching them more about prayer, he used this story: "Suppose you went to a friend's house at midnight, wanting to borrow three loaves of bread. You say to him, 'A friend of mine has just arrived for a visit, and I have nothing for him to eat.' And suppose he calls out from his bedroom, 'Don't bother me. The door is locked for the night, and my family and I are all in bed. I can't help you.' But I tell you this—though he won't do it for friendship's sake, if you keep knocking long enough, he will get up and give you whatever you need because of your shameless persistence.

"And so I tell you, keep on asking, and you will receive what you ask for. Keep on seeking, and you will find. Keep on knocking, and the door will be opened to you. For everyone who asks, receives. Everyone who seeks, finds. And to everyone who knocks, the door will be opened.

PHOTO CREDITS

Parable of the Plants:
Cover: @arthon meekodong via Canva.com
Plowing field: @Avalon_Studio via Canva.com
Planting seeds: @SimonSkafar via Canva.com
Seeds: @icon0.com via Canva.com
Sparrows: @petrovaliliya via Canva.com
Dying flower: @Ernest Tse via Canva.com
Thorns: @gonzalo martinez via Canva.com
Healthy crop: @Pgiam via Canva.com
Squirrel: @JZHunt via Canva.com
Deep roots: @Mieke Townsend via Canva.com
Stuck sheep: @ALJ1 via Canva.com
Cross: @Booneyachoat via Canva.com
Bounty: @AtWaG via Canva.com

Son who Strayed:
Cover: Photo by Josh Hild: https://www.pexels.com/photo/back-view-of-a-man-walking-in-the-train-tracks-5550027/
Money: @Nikolodian via Canva.com
Suitcase: @mikkelwilliam via Canva.com
Empty pocket: @anurakpong via Canva.com
Pig slop: @Sonya Kate Wilson via Canva.com
Feast: @LauriPatterson via Canva.com
Binoculars: @Brand X Pictures via Canva.com
Sorry: @ImagineGolf via Canva.com
Steaks: @AlexRaths via Canva.com
Angry: @Shora Shimazaki from Pexels via Canva.com
Confused: @Science Photo Library via Canva.com
Sunset: @amriphoto via Canva.com
Embrace: @triloks via Canva.com

Law Looks at Love & Life:
Cover: @towfiqu barbhuiya via Canva.com
Hourglass: @banusevim via Canva.com
Neighbors: @Quality Stock Arts via Canva.com
Jericho: ID49893740 © Victor Belokrinitski |Dreamstime.com
Injured: @paolaroid via Canva.com
Leader: @Manuel F O via Canva.com
Temple worker: @UntitledImages via Canva.com

Law Looks at Love & Life (cont.):
Mule: @Luke1138 via Canva.com
Oil: @Rido via Canva.com
Hotel: @Lucas Andrade from Pexels via Canva.com
Coins: @ma-no via Canva.com
Choice: @wildpixel via Canva.com

The Shepherd and the Sheep:
Cover: @JimSchemel via Canva.com
Discussion: @Rafiico Studio via Canva.com
Discussion: @bimsuakiemtien via Canva.com
Sheep: @Lukas from Pexels via Canva.com
Stray: @mladensky via Canva.com
Shock: @Dan Hamill from Pexels via Canva.com
Lost: @membio via Canva.com
Treacherous: @chrislebiecki via Canva.com
Count: @panoramka via Canva.com
Sheepfold: @panoramka via Canva.com
Shoulders: @Katakam Swai Swaroop from Pexels via Canva.com
Home: @panoramka via Canva.com
Celebration: @kokoroyuki via Canva.com
Shalom: @eyefocusaz via Canva.com

The King's Banquet:
Cover: Sergeykond via Canva.com
Idea List: @marekuliasz via Canva.com
Checklist: @mills21 via Canva.com
Excuses: @silvrshootr via Canva.com
Land: @Mark Plötz from Pexels via Canva.com
Cows: @tilo via Canva.com
Wife: @Leah Kelley from Pexels via Canva.com
Cross: @woolzian via Canva.com
Handicapped: @AndreyPopov via Canva.com
    @Helgy via Canva.com
    @Eleonora_os via Canva.com
    @Shannon Fagan via Canva.com
    @cottonbro studio from Pexels via Canva.com
Tables: ID 6452128 © Dallaseventsinc | Dreamstime.com
Outskirts: @givagaphotos via Canva. Com
Crowd: @photografiaBasica via Canva.com
Open hands: @rattanakun via Canva.com

The Wheat and the Weeds:
Cover: ID 42856758 © Rsooll | Dreamstime.com
Plowed: @demachi via Canva.com
Moon: @sandid from Pixabay via Canva.com
Weeds: @Sezaryadigar via Canva.com
Wheat field: @Marholev via Canva.com
Wheat: @Marccophoto via Canva.com
Ripe wheat: @mareandmare via Canva.com
Winnowing: @Ali Çobanoglue via Canva.com
Son of Man: ID21013882 © Mike_kiev |Dreamstime.com
Globe: @jaminwell via Canva.com
Unwavering: @studioroman via Canva.com
Weed bag: @hamikus via Canva.com
World's end: @Alan Godfrey via Canva.com
Angels: @bestdesigns via Canva.com

Smart Versus Silly:
Cover: @Serhii Yevkokymov via Canva.com
Saying Yes: @PeteWill via Canva.com
Embarrassed: @gurinaleksandr via Canva.com
Sleepy Cat: @WelshPixie from Pixabay via Canva.com
Splitting paths: @Sjo via Canva.com
Conflict: @Galina Sharapova via Canva.com
Sorrow: @RichLegg via Canva.com
Exhausted: @Andrea Piacquadio from Pexels via Canva.com
Leviticus: @rick734's Images via Canva.com
Sermon: https://pixabay.com/illustrations/christ-faith-sermon-on-the-mount-4852596/ @geralt
Rocks: ID105977544 © Martin Holden |Dreamstime.com
Collapsed: @ImagineGolf via Canva.com
Teaching: @rick734's Images via Canva.com
East West: @shihina via Canva.com
Strength: @nuvisionphotography via Canva.com
Straight: @gilas via Canva.com
Love: @baza178 via Canva.com
Peace: @Imagesbybarbara via Canva.com
Surrender: @tolgart via Canva.com

Local Laborers Meet Liberal Landowner:
Cover: @BenGoode via Canva.com
Sunrise: @Ville Heikkinen via Canva.com
Checklist: @Devonyu via Canva.com
Worker: @Jacob Lund via Canva.com

Local Laborers Meet Liberal Landowner (cont.):
Clock: @LFO62 via Canva.com
Workers: @pixeldigits via Canva.com
Sunset: @Summer Stock from Pexels via Canva.com
Payment: @gabrielabertolini via Canva.com
In hand: @momentstock via Canva.com
Hot work: @iluhanos via Canva.com
Handshake: @GCShutter via Canva.com
Finger people: ID 235477084 © Mukhina1 Dreamstime.com

Two Men at the Temple:
Cover proud: @khosro via Canva.com
Cover humble: @Ibrakovic via Canva.com
Keep Out sign: @AlanFalcony via Canva.com
Distaste: @DAPA Images via Canva.com
VIP: @kikkerdirk via Canva.com
Hated: @ruffraido via Canva.com
Spotlight: @robertsrob via Canva.com
Pointing: @Juan Moyano via Canva.com
Heart: @congerdesign from Pixaby via Canva.com
Tithe: @FatCamera via Canva.com
Gavel: @Creativeye99 via Canva.com
Chains: @aydinmutlu via Canva.com
Truth: @artursczcybylo via Canva.com
Thumbs down: @aluxum via Canva.com
Thumbs up: @Edmond Dantes from Pexels via Canva.com

Finding Favor with a Friend:
Cover: @PeskyMonkey via Canva.com
Praying: @anyka via Canva.com
Heaven: @darksite via Canva.com
Earth: @robertsrob via Canva.com
Feed Us: @ImagineGolf via Canva.com
Refuge: @piskunov via Canva.com
Prayer: @digitalskillet via Canva.com
Suitcases: @pixelshot via Canva.com
Knock: @cagan via Canva.com
Bed: @sevendeman via Canva.com
Firm: @AndreyPopov via Canva.com
Food: @24isk via Canva.com
Persistent: @BBuilder via Canva.com
Door: @releon8211 via Canva.com

ABOUT THE AUTHOR

Liz's mission statement as a writer (and as a person) is to be an articulate, beautiful, creative design emerging from God's heart into the jumbled kaleidoscope of lovely mankind—never overlooking people, quietly and rightly sharing truth, understanding, validating, welcoming, exalting Yahweh zealously.

She loves words! She has previously published two books of Christian poetry and one grammar workbook for middle school classrooms. She is a regular contributor to several Guideposts projects and to the Short and Sweet series by Grace Publishing.

Trained in elementary education, she loves to find ways to make learning interesting and is working on lots of projects, like picture books for younger grades and worksheets for each of the fifty states.

The idea for this paraphrase came out of her familiarity with another alliterative parable called "The Prodigal Son in the Key of F." It was written in the 1940s and has been attributed to John Garlock and Gwen Jones.

Liz and her husband have been married for forty-six years and have two children, who, along with their spouses, have provided them with four beautiful grandchildren. Her recent retirement has afforded her some long-awaited time to work on writing projects that have been in the works for a while and on brand-new ideas that the Lord drops into her spirit.

She hopes that you enjoy this fresh perspective on the words of Jesus, whether you are already familiar with them from reading the scriptures or they are brand-new stories to you.

May God bless you and fill you with His lovely gifts however that looks in your life.

SPECIAL THANKS TO...

My Minnesota Christian Writer's Guild critique group—you encouraged me through the process of writing alliteratively. Barb Winfield and Penny Moga, I'm glad you were my cheerleaders.

Jason Sisam, MCWG President and friend, for your leadership and encouragement through all of my writing projects, and especially through the navigation of self-publishing.

David Sluka, for your friendship and support and for introducing me to your wonderful graphic designer.

Yvonne Parks, for your beautiful cover design.

My children and all fifteen of their cousins—you were the inspiration for my very first parable. It was so much fun writing that gift for you that I went on to write nine more.

www.ingramcontent.com/pod-product-compliance
Lightning Source LLC
Chambersburg PA
CBHW060347090426
42734CB00011B/2062